PRAISE FOR
THE SAINT MAKERS

"Drape's latest is a feel-good account of the campaign to canonize the Rev. Emil Kapaun.... The book is at its most thrilling in its tales of the priest's wartime heroics.... Fascinating." — *The New York Times*

"Inspiring and beautifully written, Joe Drape's new book seamlessly combines three fascinating tales: the saga of a Catholic war hero and future saint, the story of how the church 'canonizes' a person (that is, recognizes saints), and the spiritual journey of an initially skeptical author. *The Saint Makers* is revelatory in truest sense of the word: it reveals Father Kapaun's astounding holiness, the church's dogged pursuit of the truth, and the author's heartfelt quest for a more authentic spiritual life."
—**James Martin, SJ, author of** *My Life with the Saints* **and** *Learning to Pray*

"In a riveting story that moves from a small town in Kansas to the halls of the Vatican, Joe Drape draws back the curtain on one of Catholicism's least-understood processes, the making of a Saint. It's a story of spiritual struggle—in prisoner-of-war camps in Korea, in the lives of modern families praying for miraculous healing, and in the personal pilgrimage of an author alienated by scandals in the Church. Drape's narrative is engaging and thought-provoking. With a combination of journalistic skepticism and religious sensitivity, he confronts the question: Why do saints matter today?"

—**John Thavis, author of** ***The Vatican Diaries***

"A phenomenal book...[Joe Drape] is a fantastic writer....He takes you through this incredible journey of an American war hero who was a Catholic priest who was so brave and patient and peaceful and kind and had so much valor and humanity."

—**Fox News's** ***Kennedy Saves the World***

"Hope and inspiration seem in short supply as this pandemic persists, but a bit of divine intervention seems to burst from Drape's new book....Resisting hagiography, he investigates the convoluted process of saint-making and the fascinating characters who gather evidence and led the campaign for Father Kapuan's sainthood. Drape enriches an inquiry into his own faith with a light personal touch, drawing on his Jesuit youth and reflecting the universal draw of Kapaun's heroism."

— ***The National Book Review***

"Engaging...this profile in sainthood is humane and compelling."   — ***Kirkus Reviews***

"An illuminating exploration of the heroism of Korean War military chaplain Emil Kapaun...[A] moving account of courage and faith in the killing fields of Korea."   — ***Publishers Weekly***

"An absorbing story....Drape...thoughtfully explor[es]

his complex relationship with his faith, burnished by his research into Fr. Kapaun.... This insightful account will appeal to readers who enjoy stories about faith and war heroics, and those interested in saint making within the Catholic Church."
— *Library Journal*

"A fascinating look into a world that for centuries has been mostly hidden...Drape [tells] the story of the saint-making process, with detail and drama...[an] extraordinary look into the previously unknown and most holy process of the Catholic Church."
— *Feisty Side of Fifty* podcast

"A fantastic read." —KSCJ's *Having Read That...*

"Joe Drape tells a compelling tale in *The Saint Makers*. Indeed, the man is a fantastic writer, and his talent is on full display....Here the book will likely prove eye-opening for the average Catholic who is unfamiliar with what it takes to get someone beatified or canonized....Drape is on a pilgrimage. Judging by what he writes here, he is growing in his faith, and his recounting of his journey is compelling, thought-provoking reading."
— *National Catholic Register*

"A great book."
—EWTN Catholic Radio's *The Miracle Hunter*

THE SAINT MAKERS

THE SAINT MAKERS

INSIDE THE CATHOLIC CHURCH AND HOW A WAR
HERO INSPIRED A JOURNEY OF FAITH

JOE DRAPE

hachette
BOOKS

NEW YORK

Cover design by LeeAnn Falciani
Cover photographs © Shutterstock: Rosary © Jakub Krechowicz; texture © VolodymyrSanych; texture © Nik Merkulov
Cover copyright © 2022 by Hachette Book Group, Inc.

All photographs courtesy of the Father Kapaun Guild except for those featuring Chase Kear and Avery Gerleman, which are courtesy of Chase Kear and family and of Avery Gerleman and family, respectively.

Robert Ellsberg, "Blessed Among Us," from *Give Us This Day: Daily Prayer for Today's Catholic* (Collegeville, MN: Liturgical Press, 2020). Excerpts used with permission.

"Ascension" from *Journey: New and Selected Poems, 1969–1999* by Kathleen Norris, © 2020. Reprinted by permission of the University of Pittsburgh Press.

Hachette Books
Hachette Book Group
1290 Avenue of the Americas
New York, NY 10104
HachetteBooks.com
Twitter.com/HachetteBooks
Instagram.com/HachetteBooks

First Trade Paperback Edition: April 2022

Published by Hachette Books, an imprint of Perseus Books, LLC, a subsidiary of Hachette Book Group, Inc. The Hachette Books name and logo is a trademark of the Hachette Book Group.

The Hachette Speakers Bureau provides a wide range of authors for speaking events.

To find out more, go to www.hachettespeakersbureau.com or call (866) 376-6591.

The publisher is not responsible for websites (or their content) that are not owned by the publisher.

Print book interior design by Sean Ford.

Library of Congress Cataloging-in-Publication Data

Names: Drape, Joe, author.
Title: The saint makers: inside the Catholic Church and how a war hero inspired a journey of faith / Joe Drape.
Description: First edition. | New York: Hachette Books, 2020. | Includes bibliographical references and index.
Identifiers: LCCN 2020030724 | ISBN 9780316268813 (hardcover) | ISBN 9780316268806 (ebook)
Subjects: LCSH: Kapaun, Emil, 1916–1951. | Catholic Church—Kansas—Pilsen—Clergy—Biography. | Military chaplains—United States—Biography. | Korean War, 1950–1953—Chaplains—United States—Biography. | Heroes—United States—Biography. | Korean War, 1950–1953—Prisoners and prisons, American. |
Classification: LCC BX4705.K2197 D73 2020 | DDC 282.092 [B]—dc23
LC record available at https://lccn.loc.gov/2020030724

ISBNs: 9780316268813 (hardcover), 9780316268820 (trade paperback), 9780316268806 (ebook)

Printed in the United States of America

LSC-C

Printing 1, 2022

To Mary & Jack
You are my answered prayers

THE SAINT MAKERS

1

It took a three-by-three-by-three-foot wooden crate crammed with 8,268 pages of documents to launch this pilgrimage from Wichita, Kansas, to Rome, Italy, and—with patience—hopefully, the Gates of Heaven. Inside was the life's work of two priests separated by fifty-seven years. Father John Hotze signed the FedEx bill, then watched as the three-hundred-pound crate was scooted onto a dolly.

He then watched his scholarship roll out the door.

It was July 2, 2011, and inside that crate was the remarkable life of Father Emil Kapaun. In the previous dozen years, Father Hotze had unearthed every letter the military chaplain and war hero had written to his family and friends back in Kansas. He had unearthed copies of the sermons Father Kapaun had given from pulpits in farm parishes as well as theaters of war. Father Hotze had the notebooks Kapaun had filled while studying to become a Catholic priest in the 1930s. Then there was the testimony of more than a hundred witnesses, from Korea to Kansas, recounting the heroics Father Kapaun had performed on the battlefield and in a prisoner-of-war camp.

But Father Hotze asked himself for the gazillionth time, Was it enough?

Father Hotze, fifty-one, was a homegrown and beefy Kansan who was more comfortable in dungarees and a work shirt than the priestly uniform of black that he was sweating through on this June morning, a day that had transformed south central Kansas into a broiler. On his drive in to the office of the Diocese of Wichita that morning, he had seen the combines vibrating in the heat as the farmers hustled to bring the wheat in before a sudden thunderstorm could render a year's work, and hundreds of thousands of dollars of investment, into drowned stalks barely worth the pennies on the insurance claim they would have to file.

Like the farmers, Father Hotze was worried about the fruits of his own harvest—the materials sown and reaped into those boxes were off to the Vatican where the contents would be measured by the most divine of standards. The life and times of Father Emil Kapaun were about to be reviewed and challenged, picked apart, and prayed over by layers of canon lawyers, Catholic cardinals, and, ultimately, the pope himself.

Father Kapaun's arc from a farm boy educated in

a one-room schoolhouse during the Depression to the most decorated chaplain in military history was compelling. His battlefield exploits were the stuff of adventure novels: He dodged the bullets of Chinese soldiers to rescue wounded Americans. He put them on his shoulders and carried them for days over frozen snow in subzero temperatures. In a North Korean prisoner-of-war camp, Father Kapaun kept hundreds of his fellow soldiers alive, and instilled the will to live in thousands more, by stealing food for their shriveled bodies and saying Mass and ministering to their crushed souls. When his captors decided they had had enough of the defiant priest, they removed him from the group. As he was carried away by stretcher—starved, sick, and unable to stand—to die alone in a fetid Death House, his fellow prisoners wept. They were Catholics and Christians, Jews and Muslims all touched deeply by this remarkable priest. Father Kapaun astonished them once more when he forgave his tormentors before them and asked them to forgive him.

What hung in the balance was a question far beyond this earth: Did this simple Kansas priest who died a horrible death in a North Korean prison camp at the age of thirty-five really belong in the Congregation of Saints? Father Hotze understood this was a pass-or-fail test. He may have looked like he should be baling hay, but Father Hotze possessed a disciplined mind that rivaled his unshakable faith.

Both priests had been forged by indecision and doubt.

Growing up in Kansas, John Hotze was a fine student and decent athlete but one who was forever adrift. He earned a business degree from Wichita State, and had done well enough to be accepted into the university's business school to pursue a master's. He cruised through his first year of studies but struggled in his second year to find motivation. Hotze detested sitting in a classroom and, after three straight semesters of enrolling in classes that he subsequently dropped after a few weeks, set out to find himself. Where? At first it didn't matter. His brother Bill was an army sergeant stationed in Germany, which was reason enough for Hotze to spend some time there and traveling through Europe.

There were more weeks spent crossing Canada by train—camping and couch surfing. When his money ran out and his curiosity needed recharging, Hotze returned to Wichita to work for his sister Mary, who had a successful business creating retail and holiday displays. They called themselves high-tack engineers and spent their days outfitting mannequins in air-conditioned malls. It earned him plenty of walking-around money, but Hotze had this nagging feeling that God had something more planned for him.

The Hotzes had faith and were practicing Catholics, but were by no means fanatics. They went to Mass as a family on Sundays and abstained from meat on Ash

Wednesday and Fridays during the Lenten season, but otherwise offered no display of public devoutness.

In their community south of Wichita, humility and discretion were the fabric that bound neighbors together. All John Hotze knew about religious vocations was what he had heard one Sunday each year when a diocesan priest took the pulpit at his parish to recruit more clergy.

Did Hotze feel a calling from God? Did he possess a vocation? He had no idea.

The Lord hadn't dumped him off a tractor and told him to change his ways as he had knocked Saul off his horse on his way to Damascus and told him to become Saint Paul. Hotze also did not know if poverty, obedience, and celibacy were the right paths to finding his true self. There wasn't anything attractive about it.

But he was twenty-eight and lost. Entering Mount Saint Mary's Seminary in Emmitsburg, Maryland, did not seem like the dumbest idea in the world. He figured either it would last only a few weeks before he tired of yet another school or God would tell him what do.

Five years later, in 1993, John Hotze was ordained. His first assignment was at All Saints Parish in Wichita, the same church he grew up in and where the Hotze family spent their Sundays. He was at home for two years before being reassigned to St. John Nepomucene in Pilsen, Kansas, where Father Kapaun had not only grown up but had also once been the pastor. Father Hotze had heard the stories of Father Kapaun's virtue and valor—most people in these parts of Kansas had. Hotze's mother had kept a prayer card tucked in a corner of the bathroom mirror depicting Father Kapaun, and the family asked often for his help when a crisis was upon them.

Father Hotze had prayed to Father Kapaun often while in university and seminary, asking him to intercede when he grew bored and restless and wanted to drop out. Father Hotze had not only finally finished what he started, but now he also had a flock who looked to him for guidance. His superiors in the chancery—the home office—soon recognized that Father Hotze might have more to offer the diocese. He was a bright guy with a burning curiosity as well as a nice touch with ordinary people. Father Hotze, then thirty-five, also had maturity and worldliness by virtue of being a seeker who was late to his calling. Bishop Eugene Gerber, the man in charge, advised Father Hotze to go to The Catholic University of America in Washington, DC, where he could pursue a JCL (*Juris Canonici Licentiatus*) in canon law, which is the highly specialized, some say Byzantine, legal system that creates and enforces the laws of the Roman Catholic Church. Byzantine or not, canon law is part of the business of diocesan and parish affairs: someone in the Wichita area needed to know how to interpret and apply its rules.

Father Hotze wasn't sure why a priest perfectly happy serving farm communities needed an advanced degree to administer what Thomas Aquinas, the Church's greatest thinker and philosopher, had foreseen as "an ordinance of reason for the common good" enacted by "competent authority." He decided the most prudent course, however, was to do as he was told—so he tucked the frayed Father Kapaun prayer card of his mother's into his black suit coat and headed to Washington, DC.

Over the next two years, both Father Kapaun and that prayer card got a workout, never more so than on the days leading to his final test. Father Hotze needed to pass a Spanish exam. Easy, huh? Not for him. Foreign languages were his most glaring weaknesses. He had already taken the translation test twice before; he had flamed out. So Father Hotze prayed hard to Father Kapaun, as did his classmates who knew of his devotion to the Kansas chaplain. They stood outside the classroom where he was taking the test with bowed heads and closed eyes and asked that Father Kapaun intercede on their friend's behalf.

Father Hotze did his best and turned in his test to the instructor. What was done was done. His academic fate was now in God's hands. He headed out to join his classmates for a beer at happy hour in their favorite saloon to celebrate their shared academic achievement. Father Hotze did not get far. Monsignor Green, the head of the language department, caught him on the steps of the building and asked for a word.

"Are you going on for a PhD?" the professor asked.

"No," said Father Hotze, "this is it for me."

The professor narrowed his eyes.

"Good," the monsignor said. "You got maybe two translations right, but I'm going to pass you. Don't ever let me see you back here again."

Father Hotze was awarded his JCL, a degree that he still believed he had no use for (and nearly didn't acquire), and returned to Kansas. He was sent to Newton, a town of no more than nineteen thousand, north of Wichita, to become the pastor at Our Lady of Guadalupe Parish. For four years, no one ever asked him a single question about canon law.

In the fall of 2001, however, Father Hotze was summoned to the chancery by Bishop Thomas Olmsted, who had just been elevated to the rank of bishop and was overseeing a diocese for the first time. He was a fellow Kansan, and he held a doctorate in canon law from Pontifical Gregorian University in Rome, Italy, which was created in the sixteenth century by Saint Ignatius of Loyola, the founder of the Jesuit order. Bishop Olmsted's intellect was matched by his ambition: he had been an official in the Vatican Secretariat of State for more than a decade in Rome. Bishop Olmsted asked Father Hotze what he knew about Father Kapaun.

Father Hotze told him about his deep devotion to the priest, and they shared a laugh at how Father Kapaun had interceded in his Spanish test. Bishop Olmsted was contemplating a campaign to have the hero of the Kansas plains presented to the Vatican's Congregation for the Causes of Saints to be considered for sainthood. He had a job for Father Hotze for the cause of Father Kapaun, one with a fancy title: Episcopal Delegate. Bishop Olmsted was not the first Catholic clergyman to champion Father Kapaun. It was not a new thought—the Archdiocese for the Military Services had first taken up his cause, and, in 1993, Father Kapaun cleared the first step on the road to sainthood when Pope John Paul II declared him a Servant of God. But a campaign for sainthood demands money and manpower. Both had been in short supply, so the cause of Father Kapaun had stalled.

Bishop Olmsted told Father Hotze that it was a long, costly process but that he was willing to invest hundreds of thousands of the diocese's money into the effort. He also assured Hotze that neither one of them would be alive when—or if—Father Kapaun was ever canonized. The plan was to launch the campaign and leave it in the best shape possible for whichever bishop, priest, and postulator came after them.

The numbers made that a very good bet. Since 1588, when the Vatican started keeping records on the process, the average time between the death of an eventual saint and canonization was 181 years. Even more daunting was the dearth of American-born saints: there were only two, Saint Elizabeth Ann Seton and Saint Katharine Drexel. Sister Seton founded the first American order of nuns, the Sisters of Charity, as well as the nation's first Catholic elementary school, which as luck would have it, was adjacent to Mount Saint Mary's Seminary, where Father Hotze earned his divinity degree. Sister Drexel was an heiress and philanthropist who founded the Sisters of the Blessed Sacrament. She was canonized in the year 2000, after thirty-four years of consideration.

On this sweltering July afternoon in the offices of the Diocese of Wichita, Kansas, however, the long odds Father Kapaun faced in becoming a saint was out of the hands of Father Hotze. For a dozen years, he had dug in and put his shoulder into a process that at first intimidated him, at times plummeted him into doubt and despair, but ultimately deepened his faith.

With Bishop Olmsted's campaign in mind, Father Hotze allowed himself a moment of triumph, an ever so brief one. The day before at a Mass and ceremony at the Cathedral of the Immaculate Conception in downtown Wichita, Father Hotze and the diocese officially celebrated the closing of their investigation into Father Kapaun's worthiness.

Now they were handing off his cause to an Italian canon lawyer by the name of Dr. Andrea Ambrosi. He was the postulator for Father Kapaun, the man who would argue the case in the Vatican for why the priest should become a saint. It was Ambrosi who would take the spadework of Father Hotze and transform it into a *Positio super vita, virtutibus et fama sanctitatis*—or Statement on the Life, Virtue, and Holy Reputation of this Servant of God.

Dr. Ambrosi was charged with crafting Hotze's finding into a narrative (in Italian, of course) and becoming the chief spokesman and lobbyist for Father Kapaun in Vatican City. The diocese felt fortunate to have Ambrosi. For generations, his family was part of the Vatican machinery, and he was considered a go-to postulator in Rome. He had spent thirty-seven years burnishing the lives of would-be saints and investigating hundreds of reported miracles they had allegedly bestowed over the globe.

Besides Father Kapaun, Ambrosi was working on a dozen other candidates, including Archbishop Fulton Sheen, a leading theologian and outsized personality who was America's first televangelist. In fact, Archbishop Sheen had won two Emmy Awards for bringing matters of faith into our homes in the early days of television. Ambrosi had come to Wichita for the Mass and ceremony for Father Kapaun, looking immaculate, old-world, and elegant in a bespoke suit. He was all those things—as well as expensive. The average cost of a cause for sainthood was half a million dollars, and the billable hours of Ambrosi would eat up much of that. At the foot of the altar, amber and rouge light reflected through the stained glass and spotlighted the wood crate. After the box was sealed with red wax, Ambrosi tied a red ribbon around it.

Afterward, Ambrosi was upbeat about the chance Father Kapaun had for measuring up to the near-impossible standards of the Congregation of Saints.

"I'm not worried," he said in Italian (as translated by his assistant).

He ticked off a highlight reel of the sacrifices and the derring-do Father Kapaun had performed on the battlefield. He nodded to the detail and testaments from fellow soldiers who Father Hotze had chased down and brought to life.

Two miracles would have to be attributed to Father Kapaun to get him over the finish line, and Ambrosi believed that he might have two already in his pocket from right here in Kansas.

In 2006, a girl named Avery Gerleman, then twelve, spent eighty-seven days in the hospital and doctors told her parents that they had exhausted all medical options. Her parents remained devoted to Father Kapaun, praying to him day and night and enlisting their friends in their parish to do the same. Avery was on a ventilator, her kidneys were failing, and, finally, doctors decided to induce a coma. Her organs were ravaged. If Avery was to live at all, doctors believed, it would be in a vegetative state. Little by little, Avery appeared to heal herself. Sixth months later, she was back on the soccer field. Two years later, Chase Kear, a college track athlete, fractured his skull from ear to ear in a pole vaulting accident. His brain bled and doctors told his family that his chances to survive surgery bordered between slim and none. Kear's family and friends petitioned to Father Kapaun. The young man survived the surgery and was out of the hospital eight weeks later. Doctors in both cases said there was no medical explanation for either of their recoveries: they had witnessed miracles.

After decades of promoting the causes of priests and nuns, Ambrosi especially relished the task of arguing for a hero like Father Kapaun who had impacted so many lives far beyond the borders of their parishes.

"He saved so many people's lives, lived his final days in a prison camp, died so young," Ambrosi said of Father Kapaun. "Already by itself, it all says something great about him that you don't need to read. You know it. He showed that there was not just a devil working on the battlefields of the war, but something else."

Now in the diocese office, Father Hotze couldn't help but think back to a letter Kapaun had written to a family friend on the eve of his ordination. This had been one of Father Hotze's early discoveries, and, as he'd read it, he had felt like Father Kapaun was talking to him.

"I feel like the dickens," Kapaun wrote. "Maybe you do not realize fully what it means to be a priest, but I tell you—after I have studied all these years, I am more convinced that a man must be a living saint in order to take that step. And that is where my worries come in. Gee whiz, I have a feeling that I am far, far from being a saint."

Father Hotze, on the other hand, believed with every cell in his body that Father Kapaun was a saint. He bowed his head and prayed that he had done enough to make the case to Rome, to the pope, and to the world that this priest did indeed deserve sainthood. And he fervently hoped that those 8,268 pages of documents would convince them.

2

It was early morning and Rome was still sleeping as I walked alongside the Tiber River on my way to the Congregation for the Causes of Saints. Tourists were lining up outside St. Peter's Basilica and the Vatican museums. They are home to priceless works of art, from the frescoes of the Sistine Chapel and Michelangelo's ceiling to the ancient Laocoön sculpture animating a moment of the Trojan War. With its treasures and its cultural and historical significance, it is easy to overlook the fact that Vatican City is a company town. As a Catholic, it is my company's town. It is the headquarters of the multibillion-dollar Catholic Church. It is the kingdom of a monarchy with Pope Francis as its head. It is where the spiritual, ecclesiastical, and commercial sausage gets made. Vatican City is not much different than Washington, DC, when it comes to government, or New York City when it comes to Wall Street.

It is far more exclusive than most, however, with eight hundred or so denizens in a city of roughly 0.17 square mile. Most of them are in uniform—the clergy in their black pants or cassocks and white collars who keep the business of spirituality humming; and the Pontifical Swiss Guard who look like peacocks in their tricolor blue, red, and yellow dress uniforms, and who are there to protect. Vatican City's demographics skew older, and the apartments inhabited by the Catholic Church's higher-ranking officials are prime real estate with old-world charm. Each morning another two thousand or so bureaucrats and administrators, engineers, and mainte-nance workers arrive, puffing up Vatican City's chest and assisting in matters of policy and commerce.

On this morning, I was stopping outside its walls at the Congregation for the Causes of Saints to meet with Monsignor Robert Sarno. He was an American, a New Yorker actually, who had been a part of the Saint-making machinery for nearly forty years. I had been told that Monsignor Sarno answered his own phone, and I was also forewarned that he was a gruff, blunt man who did not suffer fools easily. My briefers were correct on both counts. I had called the monsignor the prior week and he picked up the phone on its second ring. He was not eager to see me because he was a stickler for process and I had not gone through proper channels. Still, he agreed to a brief meeting after I pleaded ignorance of the protocols and explained that I was in Rome already.

I promised him that I would not take up much of his time.

I got crossways with the monsignor as soon as I took a chair across from his desk.

"Where in New York do you live?" he asked.

"The city," I answered.

"I'm from Brooklyn—that's part of the city," he said. "Are you from Brooklyn?"

"Manhattan," I said, chastened.

In a bid to better break the ice, I asked about the painting behind his desk of Mary and the baby Jesus. "Is that famous or have some particular meaning?"

"No, it's just a picture I liked. What can I help you with?" he asked.

Knowing my time was limited, I explained that I understood the steps of becoming a saint and was familiar with the machinery in place here in Rome, but I was interested in what he believed was at the essence of a saint.

Monsignor Sarno inched up in his seat and launched into an explanation that he had leaned on often in interviews with others. He said the Lord, only for reasons he knows, chooses some people in certain moments of history and bestows gifts on them. These gifts are witnessed by the people in his or her community at the time and are interpreted as "sign posts" on a road, and they lay out a path to follow in life or for how to get to heaven. In saints, Monsignor Sarno explained, word of these gifts spreads beyond the community and is handed down for generations. At some point, these gifts become widely known. People start praying for this gifted and holy person to help them and, if the person possesses the stuff of saints, miracles occur—people come out of comas or diseases suddenly disappear without medical explanation.

"I like to say that a saint has two I's," he said, warming up. "The 'I' for imitation and the 'I' for intercession. Once a bishop has determined that the faithful is convinced of this 'imitatableness' if you will, and then has the confirmation that prayers have been answered through the intercession of these individuals, he can start a process, the cause."

In a few quick strokes, Monsignor argued that Saint making is among the most democratic processes because the causes bubble up from the Church faithful. It takes time because reams of evidence must be discovered, and scores of historians and theologians—experts all—must examine the candidate's life and alleged miracles. When that is concluded, the Congregation for the Causes of Saints only makes a recommendation.

"The Holy Father alone has the final decision," he said.

I asked about the importance of lobbying, politics, and even "star power." After all, John Paul II, a man whom he had worked for, was canonized in 2014, or just nine years after his death. On the day of his funeral hundreds of thousands overstuffed St. Peter's Square and chanted

"*Santo, subito*" or "Sainthood, now!" Soon after, Pope Benedict XVI waived the five-year waiting period after a person's death to begin canonization. John Paul II had previously curtailed the waiting period from fifty years to five years.

Monsignor Sarno was not biting. And what about the "cold causes," in Saint-making parlance, or the candidacies that go dormant for generations or die altogether?

He got up from behind his desk. My time was up.

"You have to find the miracles they are responsible for," he said. "The way you do that is with more prayer."

The Catholic Church teaches that all people in heaven are saints, but that canonized Saints are recognized for living lives of such heightened virtue that they are worthy of our imitation. Think of them as the superheroes of the Catholic Church. They are the first among equals in what is known as the communion of saints, or the spiritual solidarity that welds the faithful here on earth, the souls in purgatory—in Catholic doctrine, purgatory is sort of a waiting room of suffering some souls go through before ascending to heaven—and all those of truth and love, in whom the Holy Spirit is at work. There are about ten thousand saints, though the exact number and legitimacy of some of them is open to debate. The first mention of saints appeared in the fourth century. Early Christian communities venerated them in bunches mostly on reputation—all that was needed was permission from a bishop or a holy man or woman. By the sixth century, Saint Gregory of Tours, a historian and hagiographer, wrote a book on contemporary saints that were mostly clergy and ascetics. The subset of ascetics and hermits can make for some strange reading but shows that early Catholics were far more inclusive than the modern Church. Among these early saints was Saint Monegundis, the only woman in the book, and someone Gregory knew. She was married and had two daughters who died suddenly. She fell into a depression and her grief was threatening her mindfulness of God. So, with her husband's blessing, she enclosed herself in a cell with a single window. She ate bread and water and slept on the floor. Soon, other women sought her spiritual advice and that tiny cell became the cornerstone of a convent. By Saint Gregory's account, Monegundis's life of denial and prayer made space in her heart for a sacred power to cure bodies and spirits. Even after her death, those who visited her tomb were able to "drink in the resurrection."

By the seventeenth century, however, Catholic scholars found there was little historic evidence for the lives and exploits of most of these early saints. Saint Jude, one of the original twelve apostles, endures among Catholics and beyond as the patron of "hopeless causes." No one really knows why. Beyond being listed as an apostle, he is quoted only once in the Gospel of St. John, asking Jesus why he does not show himself to the whole world. He supposedly wrote the Letter of Jude, the shortest book in the New Testament, but its twenty-five verses warn against false teachers and how they can divide the Church. Nevertheless, the entertainer Danny Thomas and his actress daughter Marlo have piggybacked on Saint Jude's reputation to do the impossible and raised money and awareness for the St. Jude Children's Research Hospital in Memphis, Tennessee, which is widely considered one the finest facilities of its kind.

Some of the Church's most enduring saints were based on legends. Saint Christopher, the patron saint of travel and whose medal hangs around countless necks, was apparently a large man who was told by a hermit, as the story goes, that the best way for him to serve God and his community was by helping them cross a raging river. Basically, he became a human ferry service. One day, a small child showed up and asked Christopher to carry him across the river on his back. As they crossed, the small boy's weight became staggeringly heavy and Christopher barely was able to get him to shore. As he collapsed, the boy told him why it had been so difficult.

"You had on your shoulders not only the whole world but Him who made it. I am Christ your king, whom you are serving by this work," said the child, according to Jacobus de Voragine, who compiled *The Golden Legend*, one of the most popular books of the Middle Ages.

He wrote of Christopher: "He bore Christ in four ways, namely, on his shoulders when he carried him across the river, in his body by mortification, in his mind by devotion, and in his mouth by confessing Christ and preaching him."

Then there is the story of Saint Guinefort, who was venerated by locals near Lyon, France, and was considered the patron saint for the protection of infants after saving the son of a knight. Legend has it that upon returning to his castle one day, the knight found that his child was missing. The boy's bed was overturned and there was Guinefort with blood on his face. The knight, thinking that his babysitter had harmed his son, dispatched Guinefort with his sword. Then the knight heard a child cry. Beneath the bed, he found his boy safe—but next to him was a dead viper.

Alas, Saint Guinefort was a dog.

As the Middle Ages were ending, popes claimed the power of making a Saint was one they solely held. In 993, Saint Ulrich of Augsburg was the first saint to be formally canonized by Pope John XV. By the twelfth century, the Church centralized the process with the pope in charge of the committees that investigated and documented candidates' lives. In 1588, Pope Sixtus V created the Congregation of Rites and Ceremonies and put those individuals in charge of vetting potential candidates. When Alban Butler—a priest and professor of philosophy and theology—published the first of his four volumes of *The Lives of the Fathers, Martyrs, and Other Principal Saints* in 1756, civilization now had an organized and somewhat up-to-date guide to who was a saint and how they had become one. It took Father Butler more than thirty years to research and write about in his volumes the more than sixteen hundred men and women who were canonized. The book, now called *Lives of the Saints*, was read by future saints and continues to be revised. It has contributed to our understanding of the Catholic Church and some of its divine inspirations.

Saint-making continued to evolve. In 1969, the Congregation for the Causes of Saints—the office Monsignor Sarno served—was created by Pope Paul VI. At the same time, the pope also conducted a disciplined review of the saints already on the Church's books and put limitations on the ones found to have little evidence of their existence and the miracles that they were credited with but were never verified. They were left off the Roman calendar and no new parishes could be opened under their name.

It was John Paul II, in 1983, who relaxed the Saint-making standards by eliminating the office of the Promoter of the Faith. This office was represented by a canon lawyer, popularly known as the devil's advocate, who argued *against* a possible canonization. John Paul II changed the character of the process from a litigious exercise to a more cooperative affair. He also reduced the number of miracles required to be canonized from four to two. Don't get me wrong—it is still not easy to become a saint.

The result of this evolution is the four-step journey to sainthood in place today, the one that Father Kapaun, and other would-be saints, are undergoing. The first step is being named Servant of God. In the case of Father Kapaun, this occurred in 1993 when the diocese in Kansas opened his cause. The Congregation for the Causes of Saints reviews the *Positio super vita, virtutibus et fama sanctitatis* (Statement on the Life, Virtue, and Holy Reputation). In the case of Father Kapaun, Father Hotze researched the material for the statement and Dr. Ambrosi wrote it. The congregation is looking for evidence that Father Kapaun lived the theological, cardinal, and other virtues to a heroic degree. If the congregation finds that he did, it will issue a Decree of Heroic Virtue, giving Father Kapaun the title Venerable. Next up is beatification, or Blessed, which is a statement that declares it is worthy of belief that the candidate for sainthood is in heaven. This will allow southeast Kansas to honor Father Kapaun officially by assigning and celebrating a "feast day" where special prayers at Mass are offered. It also will allow images of Father Kapaun to be displayed inside churches. To be beatified, a single miracle must be attributed to the candidate's intercession after his or her death, providing supernatural evidence that the candidate is with God. For martyrs, or people who die for their faith, John Paul II waived the miracle clause.

Finally, for a candidate to be canonized and take his or her place at the top tier of the communion of saints, another miracle must be found to occur *after* his or her beatification. The reason? It demonstrates that God, indeed, approves this step. Is it any wonder that the average march to sainthood from death to canonization is 181 years?

So, after leading exemplary lives, being powered by the infinite prayers of the faithful, and performing real-life authenticated miracles, what do the demographics of the canonized Saints look like? Very heavy on priests and nuns and popes—90 percent in fact.

On April 27, 2014, John Paul II and John XXIII became the seventy-ninth and eightieth heads of the Church to become saints, and the first popes in the more than two-thousand-year history of the Church to be canonized on the same day. Starting with Saint Peter, its first leader after the death of Christ, fifty of the first fifty-five popes were canonized. In the last thousand years, however, only seven popes have been made Saints. Not quite there yet, but in the pipeline, are Pius IX, who died in 1878; Pius XII (1958); and John Paul I (1978), who reigned as pope for just thirty-three days before his unexpected death.

The canonizations of John Paul II and John XXIII, however, were not without controversy. John Paul II reigned for nearly twenty-seven years before his death in 2005 and became the most visible pope in history by traveling to 129 countries—more than all his predecessors combined. He had critics, however, who believed he was slow to recognize the gravity of the sexual abuse crisis in the Church that was exploding at the end of his tenure. They were especially troubled about what they perceived as the blind eye that he had for Father Maciel, the Mexican founder of a disgraced Catholic religious order, the Legionaries of Christ. Maciel was proven to be a pedophile, womanizer, and drug addict, but he had founded a rich and conservative order that John Paul II and his aides praised as the embodiment of leadership.

It was Pope Francis who decided to canonize John XXIII along with John Paul II. In doing so, he effectively waived the requirement for miracles because only one had been vetted and accepted for the beloved pope. Instead, Pope Francis declared that John XXIII's "fame of holiness" was enough to make him a saint. It was quite an exception to the rule, but it did illustrate that a pope, as the highest member of the Church, could rule as he liked on many issues.

John XXIII was named pope in 1958 and was considered a compromise candidate. He had earned the reputation of the "good pope" for his gentle kindness and an easy sense of humor. When he was once asked how many people worked in the Vatican, he memorably answered: "About half of them."

Pope John XXIII, however, made Catholicism more modern and compassionate when he called the Second Vatican Council from 1962 to 1965. It was the first meeting of the world's bishops in nearly a century and resulted in contemporary vernacular replacing Latin in the Masses, encouraged dialogue with other religious leaders, and renounced Jewish collective guilt, which is the concept that Jews should feel guilt for the death of Jesus.

Of the rosters of saints, it's not surprising (perhaps because of the home-field advantage) that Italians are the most represented, making up 46.7 percent of them, according to a 2010 research paper titled the "Economics of Sainthood (A Preliminary Investigation)" by three economists, two from Harvard and one from Columbia. Considering the glacial pace of making Saints, the numbers compiled by Robert J. Barro, Rachel M. McCleary, and Alexander McQuoid mostly hold true today. Non-Italians from Western Europe account for 33.8 percent of saints; from Eastern Europe 6.6 percent; Asia-Pacific 2.2 percent; Africa 0.7 percent; Latin America 6.6 percent; and North America 3.3 percent.

Among their other findings were that beatifications and canonizations in Western Europe, including Italy, picked up from the seventeenth century to 1950. But since then, there has been a trend toward making more Saints in other parts of the world, which is, they write, "possibly linked to the rising competitive threat from Evangelicalism." In Latin America, for example, the share of saints rose from 0 percent from 1900 to 1949, to 7 percent from 1950 to 1979, and peaked at 14 percent in the 2000s. Nearly half of the world's Catholics live in

Latin America, but the Catholic Church continues to lose market share there to the evangelical movement, which has flooded the area with lay ministers and missionaries. In 1900, Protestants accounted for 2.2 percent of the population; in 2010, that number was 16.4 percent. The Catholic share of the population, meanwhile, dropped from 90.4 percent to 82.2 percent largely because the lack of priests in the region made it hard for the Catholic Church to compete with the push of the evangelicals.

Generally, the researchers found about 80 percent of the saints had formal schooling and 96 percent were literate. Eighty percent were from urban areas. Their average age at death was sixty-two years old. The share of married saints was small—8 to 9 percent—and that low percentage was largely because priests and nuns usually have the money and muscle of their religious order to press their causes. Married priests and nuns have been rare throughout history, and saintly ones rarer still.

One thing that is clear from this research as well as from recent headlines is that our most recent contemporary popes have not been shy about adding to the roll of saints. In fact, John Paul II was an enthusiastic Saint maker, canonizing 482 of them. In his eight-year tenure, Pope Benedict XVI made 45 Saints, due to the numerous beatified (Blessed) candidates John Paul II left behind. And Pope Francis, in his first canonization, bestowed sainthood on the Martyrs of Otranto—all 813 of them— 533 years after they were beheaded by Ottoman soldiers for refusing to convert to Islam. Collectively, John Paul II, Pope Benedict XVI, and Pope Francis canonized 1,375 Saints, a number that far exceeds the total of saints, 302, canonized from 1588 to 1978.

How come? It is good for business—fiscally as well as spiritually. John Paul II went so far as to say the bar for sainthood could be cleared by all of us.

"This ideal of perfection must not be misunderstood as if it involved some kind of extraordinary existence, possible only for a few 'uncommon heroes' of holiness," he wrote in *Novo Millennio ineunte*, a 2001 apostolic letter laying out the Church's future. "The ways of holiness are many, according to the vocation of each individual. I thank the Lord that in these years he has enabled me to beatify and canonize a large number of Christians, and among them many lay people who attained holiness in the most ordinary circumstances of life."

The United States, of course, is a young country and, like in our civilization and culture, we were late to the Saint-making party. In 1884, causes were opened for Isaac Jogues and René Goupil, French missionaries and martyrs who worked with the Iroquois and Huron tribes in the early 1600s; and Tekakwitha, baptized in the late 1600s as Catherine when she was nineteen, and who became known as Lily of the Mohawks. Because the missionaries and Lily of the Mohawks did their work mostly in what is now Canada, and before the United States was its own country, their candidacy did not feel authentic to the faithful in the United States. In fact, until 1908, the United States was considered a "missionary territory" by the Church. The trio were eventually canonized—Jogues and Goupil in 1930 by Pope Pius XI and Tekakwitha in 2012 by Pope Benedict XVI. But they were not homegrown enough for American Catholics to call their own.

Neither Americans nor the Vatican were truly engaged in making an American Saint until after World War I when the country asserted itself as a power on the battlefield and a player on the world's political stage. Why shouldn't Rome recognize the US as a player and take our candidates for sainthood seriously?

By the 1930s, the US had four cardinals compared to the single one who was in place at the time Jogues, Goupil, and Tekakwitha's bids were launched in the 1880s. These four cardinals—George Mundelein in Chicago; Patrick Hayes in New York; Dennis Dougherty in Philadelphia; and William Henry O'Connell in Boston—were better organized, represented a large and devoted population of primarily immigrant Catholics, and, most important, had influence with Pope Pius XI.

"Why can't you give me an American saint?" Pope Pius XI supposedly asked one of his cardinals in the Sacred Congregation of Rites.

"I can't give you one until they give me one," the cardinal replied.

While the notion of an American saint was gaining

popularity in mainstream, secular culture—*Time* magazine suggested Notre Dame football coach Knute Rockne should be nominated—the American Catholic Church had a hard time rallying around one of the dozen or so candidates whose causes were percolating. In her book *A Saint of Our Own*, Kathleen Sprows Cummings writes that the process of recognizing saints in the United States "has often been about the ways in which Catholics defined, defended, and celebrated their identities as Americans."

That is why Mother Frances Cabrini and Bishop John Neumann moved to the front of the line. According to Cummings, they "evoked transplantation of European Catholicism rather than the conversion of native people." Both were also blessed with a memorable straight-line narrative that made it easy for supporters to stick to the talking points. Neumann, the fourth bishop of Philadelphia, was a Bohemian immigrant who spoke multiple languages. In 1842, he became the first priest from the Congregation of the Most Holy Redeemer—known as Redemptorists—in America. He championed the parochial schools and established the first parish for Italian-speaking Catholics, St. Mary Magdalen de Pazzi Roman Catholic Church. He appealed to the immigrants who swelled Philadelphia and were seeking an education and a bigger slice of the economic pie. They saw themselves in Bishop Neumann—a newcomer, building a better country for their children.

On the other side of the spectrum, Frances Cabrini, the Italian-born founder of the Missionary Sisters of the Sacred Heart of Jesus, was a champion of poverty-stricken Italian immigrants, founding hospitals and orphanages from New York to Colorado, Louisiana to Washington State. She also had pull in the Vatican. Mother Cabrini had originally planned to take her organizing skills and ministry from Italy to China. But Giovanni Battista Scalabrini, a bishop in Northern Italy, asked her to consider expanding to the United States, where Italian immigrants were pouring in. In 1877, at an audience with Pope Leo XIII, Mother Cabrini told him she could not reach a decision and asked him what she should do.

"Not to the East, but to the West," he told her.

It is little wonder perhaps that she leapfrogged all other candidates and was canonized by Pope Pius XII in 1946, just twenty-nine years after she died in 1917.

Among those candidates was Elizabeth Ann Seton, who eventually became the first American-born saint, but not until 154 years after her death. Sister Seton eluded a simple narrative, and her example was perhaps better suited for contemporary times, especially now when the Catholic Church is in conflict over how to be more inclusive. She was a Revolutionary-era Episcopalian wife, a socialite and mother of five, and then a widow. She converted, opened the first Catholic girls' school in the United States, and founded the Catholic Sisters of Charity. No one ever doubted her holiness or virtue, but her cause advanced in starts and fits. She died in 1821 at the age of forty-six, but her cause was not opened until 1907. Sometimes the complications were minor—there was trouble locating her baptism records in New York City's Trinity Church. Others were due to collateral damage to her cause by others long after her death. New York's Archbishop John Hughes—"the best known, if not exactly the best loved, Catholic bishop in the country" at the time, according to a reporter—broke up the Sisters of Charity when he forced the nuns in New York to choose between returning to the order founded by Sister Seton in Emmitsburg, Maryland, or staying in New York to continue to care for the children there. Subsequently, the order splintered into seven different groups. It hindered Seton's canonization campaign because such a campaign required, wrote Cummings, "a single story, and Seton's supporters would need to agree on one before her cause could succeed."

Seton's primary obstacle to sainthood was that she was a woman, and a woman who was not easily put into a box that appealed to an all-male bureaucracy. In fact, until the reforms made by John Paul II in 1983, women were not allowed to advocate for candidates before the Congregation for the Causes of Saints. In 1975, during a period of rising feminism and 154 years after her death, Sister Seton was made a Saint.

So there is more to Saint-making than leading a virtuous life. Enterprise and organization by a candidate's

3

Emil's father, Enos Kapaun, was fifteen years older than his wife Elizabeth. He had immigrated to the United States from Czechoslovakia as a seven-year-old in 1887 and, with his family, made a home in Pilsen, Kansas. The town was named in honor of Plzeň, a city in Bohemia, the region that the Kapauns and forty or so other families had left to start a new life in the United States. Some were Bohemian. Some were German. They settled here in Marion County, buying their land from the Atchison, Topeka and Santa Fe Railway Company, and were determined to become farmers and build families on the Great Plains of America's thirty-fourth state. It was a windswept patch of ground surrounded by a quilt of green, brown, and yellow wild grasses begging to be turned into wheat and corn and soybeans. After erecting a general store, among the community's first tasks was building a Catholic church, a practical one: a two-story frame building with the upper floor serving as the church and the lower one as a rectory.

Enos was a resourceful and tireless man with an exceptional work ethic. He made many of his own tools and was at work on his 160 acres before dawn until long after dusk. He was lean but with arms that looked like they were pulled through with steel cable. He was quiet as well. He was well into his thirties before he met twenty-year-old Elizabeth Hajek. Bessie, as she was known, was born 170 miles west of Pilsen in Trego County, but her family was from Bohemia. The couple was married by Father John Sklenar, the most important man in this hardworking, devout community, on May 18, 1915. They were in a hurry and chose not to wait for the new church to be completed. The church project was responsible for the buzz across Marion County and the never-ending pile of bricks stacking up in Pilsen. Father Sklenar had outgrown practical ambitions for it, and he was intent on building a cathedral on the plains resplendent with a 120-foot steeple. Its cornerstone had been laid the previous year, and Father Sklenar was sparing no expense—he budgeted $30,000 for materials alone knowing that he could rely on parishioners like Enos Kapaun to provide free labor. Bricks from Kansas City were arriving by train in Lincolnville, Kansas, and then hauled seven miles south to town. The brick pile got so high the running joke among townsfolk was "How many churches are you going to build?"

Enos and Bessie Kapaun wasted little time starting a family. Nine months after they married, on an unseasonably cold day, Enos and Bessie dragged a bed into the kitchen to be near the stove and keep warm as they awaited the birth of their first child. It was Holy Thursday, which the couple took as a good sign. It was the night Jesus shared His Last Supper with His disciples. The night Jesus Christ ordained his Apostles as priests. The night that he created the sacrament of the Eucharist—giving them His body and blood to eat and drink so that they could have the courage and strength to love others—so much so that they would be willing to die for them as Jesus was about to do the next day, Good Friday.

At 11:00 a.m. on April 20, 1916, Emil Joseph Kapaun was born. Four weeks later at the newly completed St. John Nepomucene, named for the patron saint of Bohemia, Father Sklenar baptized Emil into the Catholic Church.

As a young boy, Emil Kapaun fell into the rhythms of life on the plains. He followed Enos around the farm and hunted and fished with him. He was a precocious child, starting school at the age of six. He rode his bike the three miles from his home in the country to town where three nuns of the Precious Blood of Christ order taught grades one through eight in both English and Bohemian. It took him only six years to finish elementary school and he posted straight As. At home, he weeded the garden and tilled the fields. He was also in charge of the chickens and bringing in their daily eggs. Emil also possessed Enos's talent for fixing just about anything. Emil also looked after his brother, Eugene, who came along eight years after him.

Emil was like virtually every other boy in Pilsen—diligent, determined. He loved his family. He loved the outdoors and was prone to long, solitary hikes. But it was clear early on that his faith was deeper than most. As a young boy, Emil would move boxes and sawhorses to fashion makeshift altars to say make-believe Masses. He left his home for school an hour early each morning to serve as an altar boy for Father Sklenar. He was on the altar on weekends and during vacations in the summer. Shortly after Emil was confirmed on April 11, 1929, neither his parents nor Father Sklenar could deny that the boy had what was then called a vocation. He belonged in the priesthood. In September of 1930, fourteen-year-old Emil Kapaun enrolled at Conception Seminary, a boarding school and college run by Benedictine monks in Conception, Missouri. His tuition was paid for by various scholarships—at the time, most believed, there was no better investment than in a smart young man with a love for God and a passion to serve.

The Benedictines were rigorous—Emil spent two years finishing high school and another four studying Latin, Greek, and philosophy. Not only was he a star student, but he was also a generous one. He knew shorthand

and took copious notes that he then translated, mimeographed, and shared with classmates. He sang in the choir, acted in school plays, served as head librarian, and wrote for the school newspaper. Each summer, Emil returned home and worked alongside Enos, but not until he had attended Mass most days and received Holy Communion at St. John Nepomucene.

By the time he was twenty, Emil Kapaun was a handsomer version of his father Enos—he had his lean and muscled grace, sparkling eyes, and a cleft chin straight out of Hollywood. He had no interest in breaking hearts; instead he wanted to swell them with the grace of God. Father Sklenar was proud of his star pupil and recognized in him a possible successor. He went to see the Bishop of Wichita and made his case for Emil to receive diocesan funds and begin his theological studies at Kenrick Seminary in St. Louis, Missouri. The bishop agreed.

Emil Kapaun was a quick study there as well. He was made a subdeacon in the summer of 1939 and sent to Caldwell, Kansas, another German-Bohemian stronghold, where his bilingual skills were put to work, mostly as a preacher on the streets. Even as a novice, Emil connected with people by being a doer rather than a talker. He would not accost anyone abruptly or lead with his mouth. Instead, he would help a young mother carry out her goods from the general store or assist a farmer with unloading his wagon.

Then he would ask: "Do you mind if we say a little prayer?"

By Christmas, Emil was a deacon and he delivered his first sermon in Bohemian at St. John Nepomucene in his hometown. He had been baptized there, of course. He had received his first Holy Communion and had been confirmed at this cathedral on the plains. He had served countless Masses inside and now he was at the pulpit. Enos and Bessie Kapaun felt blessed and proud.

On April 6, 1940, while back in St. Louis, Emil wrote a letter to Bishop Christian Winkelmann asking to be ordained as a priest.

"In compliance with the instruction of the Sacred Congregation of the Sacrament of December 27, 1930, I humbly petition your Excellency to be promoted to the Sacred Order of Priesthood," he wrote on Kenrick Seminary stationary in a neat flowing hand.

"In presenting this petition, I solemnly declare that I am instructed by no motive of fear, either physical or moral; that I am in no way coerced by parent, pastor, assistant pastor, or any other agency whatsoever, but make this request from my own free will, and that I am fully aware of the grave obligations consequent from the reception of this Sacred Order.

"Your Excellency's most humble servant. Emil Joseph Kapaun."

On June 9, 1940, at the St. John's Chapel on the campus of Sacred Heart College in Wichita, twenty-four-year-old

Emil Joseph Kapaun was ordained by Bishop Winkelmann. It was a small, solemn affair—nothing like the joyous turnout eleven days later when Father Kapaun celebrated his first Mass. Twelve hundred denizens of Marion County, dressed in their finest suits and dresses, turned out for a procession and to receive a blessing from Father Kapaun at St. John Nepomucene. They braved the heat and long lines to kneel before the local-boy-made-divine outside the church. Father Kapaun laid his hands and a blessing on all who came before him. He wore a black cassock, a white collar, and a beatific smile as he led them into the church that many of their families had a hand in building. He had imagined this moment as a boy. He had prayed for it all his life. He had put in the study and the pastoral work. Now here he was living it out before a community that had helped him fulfill this dream. It was as monumental a day as there had ever been for the Bohemian and German farmers of Marion County.

By the end of the month, Bishop Winkelmann had assigned Father Kapaun to his hometown parish as the assistant pastor to Father Sklenar. The succession plan seemed to be in motion. In fact, when Father Sklenar retired in November 1943, Father Kapaun became the pastor of the parish that had harvested his vocation. The transition from assistant to boss, however, was a difficult one for Father Kapaun. For too many of his parishioners, he remained Enos and Bessie's boy, the little kid who had ridden his bike to church and had been the picture of piety as an altar server. They sidestepped him and sought advice and chose to unburden themselves to Father Sklenar, who had been their spiritual guide for most of their lives. Father Kapaun did find an audience and a sense of purpose working with the parish's young people. For them, Father Kapaun was half as old as Father Sklenar and twice as gentle. Father Kapaun helped with their schoolwork. He made sure they had balls and bats and baseball gloves, and he organized competitions in all sports for them. One Christmas, he gave every boy and girl a copy of the New Testament. Father Kapaun read and reread those books when he was their age. The Gospels especially were burned in his brain and offered him the only hero he ever was going to need: Jesus Christ.

But it was a side job that Bishop Winkelmann had assigned him where he found his true calling and put those New Testament lessons to work. He was appointed the auxiliary chaplain at the army air base in Herington, Kansas. On his first visit to the base, Father Kapaun knew that this was where he belonged. Like him, the soldiers were men in their twenties. Like him, they were doers—men who didn't shrink from work. They came from all over the country and were all different shapes, sizes, and ethnicities. World War II was being fought across the oceans, and the air base was bustling with soldiers shipping in and out. Father Kapaun did what he did best: he listened. It did not matter if the man was Catholic or Jewish or Baptist or atheist. It was a full-time job to hear soldiers confess their fears and talk through their doubts. He said Mass and heard confessions, but mostly he told men like him that what they were doing was appreciated by their families and their country. Sometimes he prayed with them; always he prayed for them. It did not take long for Father Kapaun to admit that he looked more forward to his part-time work on the air base than his full-time duty of trying to win over a reluctant flock in the community where he grew up. Eventually, he told Bishop Winkelmann that St. John Nepomucene needed an older, Bohemian-speaking priest. The Bishop agreed and, on July 12, 1944, recommended Father Kapaun to the US Army Chaplain Corps.

Doubts. Father Hotze had many of them when he took up Father Kapaun's cause. First, he was not sure whether he had the time or the skill set to unearth as complete an account of the life and times of Father Emil Joseph Kapaun as necessary. Sure, he was a college graduate with an advanced degree in canon law, but he also knew—and had a track record—that he could be his own worst enemy. It was not like the diocese was giving him a corner office and a staff of crack researchers, either. Father Hotze was on his own and was performing two other jobs as well that required his immediate attention. He was the pastor of St. Mary's, a parish in Newton, Kansas, thirty miles north of Wichita. He also was the judicial vicar for the diocese—a judge of sorts—who decided on cases in ecclesiastic courts. Most of his time was spent on marriage annulments—walking a previously divorced man or woman through the process of having that marriage annulled in order to have their second marriage recognized by the Catholic Church. It was time-consuming work, especially when he was trying to shoehorn it in between tending to the spiritual needs of the people of St. Mary's and trying to paint a flesh-and-bones portrait of a man, a fellow priest, that he had previously known only through a prayer card.

Narratives about the lives of saints are called hagiographies. There is a reason the word *hagiography* is often employed in the derogatory, as in to dismiss a piece of writing as being too adulatory or too idealizing toward its subject. The heroism Father Kapaun displayed in a North Korea prison camp became national news as soon as the Korean War came to an end in the summer of 1953 and his fellow prisoners were released. They told the wire service and radio reporters about the pipe-smoking Catholic priest who single-handedly kept them alive and was martyred by the Chinese and North Korean soldiers whom he openly defied. Between journalism being the "first draft of history" and it being recorded in an era when patriotism was appropriate after a brutal and bloody war, the accounts were sensational. And sensationalism sold a lot of newspapers. The stories betrayed little skepticism and helped power the legend of Father Kapaun into popular culture, earning him a profile in the *Saturday Evening Post* and an episode called "The Good Thief" on the television anthology *Crossroads*, a show that dramatized the lives of clergymen of all faiths and the problems they faced in both their professional and personal lives. Father Kapaun was played by the Oscar-nominated actor James Whitmore, who had already won a Tony Award and would later become a two-time Emmy winner.

In the earliest days of his digging, as first fatigue and then panic set in on him, Father Hotze had plenty of reasons to wonder if the story of Father Kapaun was too good to be true. So he decided to adopt a more prosecutorial style of fact-finding.

"When I realized what I was going to need to do, and with me being inherently lazy, I thought the way to go about doing this was to go out and dig up some dirt on Father Kapaun," he told me. "If I found out bad stuff about him, I could go to the bishop and say, no, we shouldn't pursue his cause."

It was an approach that led to awkward encounters with soldiers and people who knew the priest and often left Father Hotze feeling like a "schmuck." It bore fruit, though not the kind he originally intended. He would come to believe that, inherently lazy or not, there was a higher power putting him in the path of what some call luck and others call divine providence.

His first encounter with this phenomenon occurred early in his tenure at St. Mary's while he was puzzling over where exactly to start his excavation of Father Kapaun. He was interrupted by a call from the Newton Medical Center: there was a woman heading into heart surgery and the pastor of her parish was out of town. Could Father Hotze please come and pray with her and perform the anointing of the sick? He said, "Of course," and made his way to the hospital. In the woman's room, there was an elderly couple. As Father Hotze finished administering the sacrament, the man asked if he was the same Father Hotze who was working on Father Kapaun's cause. He said he was.

"I grew up with him in Pilsen," the man said.

What are the chances, he thought, that I am pinch-hitting for a fellow priest to help a woman whom I have never met at the exact same time a couple I also have never met is visiting and has a connection to Father Kapaun? Father Hotze asked about growing up with Father Kapaun. What was he like? He couldn't overtly ask for dirt on the priest, but he could attempt to poke for some holes in the priest's early life: Was he good at school?

"He was advanced twice," the man said. "We went in together, but he got out two years ahead of me."

"So he was one of those goody two-shoes?" asked Father Hotze.

"No," he replied. "But he did help everybody out. If one of us was struggling, he would know before the nuns did and go over the work with us."

"So he was teacher's pet?" asked Father Hotze.

"Nothing like that at all," the man replied. "He'd figure it out before any of the nuns knew we were in trouble. You can't believe what kind of comfort it was to have him come and help you out. You didn't have to go to the teacher and let her know you were stupid or that you just didn't understand. He helped me a bunch of times."

The initial encounters Father Hotze had with the soldiers and fellow prisoners who had served with Father Kapaun, on the other hand, were not as uplifting. They were old men in their eighties who had spent the past fifty years trying to forget the hardships and atrocities they had barely survived. He would watch their eyes go dead, their shoulders shudder, and their tears inevitably pour down their cheeks. The stories poured out, too, about shoeless overnight marches in minus-forty-degree temperatures, witnessing the agony of friends as lice chewed them to their death, or picking through fellow prisoners' feces for millet or anything that might stave off starvation for another hour or day.

When Father Hotze, seeing the pain the memories inflicted upon them, offered to stop the conversation altogether or at least resume it another time, one after another waved him off and powered on. One of them, Dr. Sidney Esensten, explained to him why: they were too haunted to talk about the horror of the experience to their wives or children and had kept it inside.

"Father, let me explain something to you," Esensten said. "I haven't slept in the same bed with my wife in fifty years. I still have nightmares. If I sleep with her, she wakes up black-and-blue because I'm thrashing around. A lot of us need to talk about this. You're the guy we can talk to."

Father Hotze listened—hour after hour, day after day.

He learned about a long-forgotten war and the hellish existence of the men who fought it. He pushed them, too. The tactic of looking for dirt on Father Kapaun may have been misguided but it wasn't wrong. Flawed men are ordinary men, and if Father Kapaun was going to be elevated to sainthood, Father Hotze understood that it was his duty to offer a 360-degree portrait of an ordinary man who, with God's grace, willed himself to do extraordinary things. He needed to be portrayed as human as he was. And as we are.

For the first time, Father Hotze had a sense of why this work had chosen him. He read it in one of the sermons Father Kapaun gave.

"Christ's work testified to what he was; our work will testify to what we are."

4

I had some doubts of my own about where Father Kapaun fit in my life. Father Hotze had been chosen to champion the cause of Father Kapaun. Even though he was partisan, his caution in the early going echoed the perspective of no less a wise man than George Orwell, who opened an essay on Mohandas Gandhi with words of caution. "Saints should always be judged guilty until they are proved innocent," he wrote in "Reflections on Gandhi."

Exploring the life of Father Kapaun and the mechanism of how the Catholic Church mints Saints was my choice. Why? At first, I thought it was simply a good story and I was perfectly capable of telling it. I was living in Smith Center, Kansas, in 2008 with my family, working on a book called *Our Boys: A Perfect Season on the Plains with the Smith Center Redmen*, when I first came across the cause of Father Kapaun and learned the bits and pieces of his backstory. I was born and raised in Kansas City, but I had not lived there for thirty years. Still, I know Kansas well, both as a child and as an adult. I have touched all four of its corners and logged many miles in the middle part of the state. What little I knew about Father Kapaun had reminded me of my neighbors in Smith Center, a town in the north central part of the state. At first, they were friendly but not overly familiar to my wife, my son, and me. In fact, they were mostly on the stoic side. The flatness of the plains, with its beiges and muted colors, can do that to you, especially when you are a farmer and spend countless hours alone in the driver's seat of a combine. It makes you solemn and serene. Like Father Kapaun, they were doers not talkers. When one family finished bringing in a harvest, they were at another's farm to help them finish up, and then on to another. Eventually, we warmed up to each other, and I consider my time in their town and the enduring friendships that have formed to be among the most cherished parts of my life.

There was a familial pull as well. My mother's family had roots in the central part of the state. My grandparents and great aunts and uncles embodied the same stolid traits—straight talking but careful not to say too much. My dad, like Father Kapaun, was a first-generation American whose parents emigrated from somewhere near Bohemia. He was orphaned in Akron, Ohio, as a young boy and either didn't know or didn't dwell on his family history.

I was Catholic, too, I guess. I went to Catholic grade school and then an all-boys Jesuit high school. Our only child, a son, has followed the same path. I like to say that he is now paying for the sins of his father with the Jesuits. Culturally, I am a Catholic at least. Growing up, my family was among the early families in our parish, Christ the King, in Kansas City. My dad served on the committee that built the rectory, our school gym and cafeteria. He ushered during Masses and was a member of the Knights of Columbus. My mom held posts on the PTA and volunteered for the bake sales and pancake breakfasts. The parents of the kids my four siblings and I grew up with were among my parents' dearest friends until their deaths. What our parents passed down to us was that the parish was about community and character. We were obligated to give back. Yes, it takes a village. They were comfortable being around people who thought the same way.

"Treat him as your own," my dad would tell my friends' folks and the nuns at school. "Even if it means knocking him through the wall."

Mom prayed the occasional novena (a nine-day-long series of prayers) and taught us to pray to Saint Anthony when we lost something ("Tony, Tony, look around, something important must be found"). But she also had earned a master's degree in social work at The Catholic

University of America and, through her work, often found herself at odds with Church doctrine. Her tenure at a home for "wayward girls," as it was then called, found her on the opposite side of its teachings on birth control, and it honed a lifelong distrust of edicts from the patriarchy. My dad, a criminal attorney, knew a lot of sinners—or at least sinners who allegedly committed a crime. He liked that our parish and our pastor had garnered the reputation as the 7-Eleven when it came to its Mass schedule because of its convenience. There were a lot of Masses, and Monsignor Vincent L. Kearney kept them short and sweet. We used to joke that after arriving five minutes late and leaving after Communion, you had put in a solid twenty-two minutes of prayer. Measured on the stovetop of devoutness, my family simmered at medium low.

Still, it was a good enough way to bring up kids that my wife and I have followed the same path. She is one of nine from an Irish American family in Chicago and, like me, remains close to a core group of her Catholic grade school and high school friends. After leaving Smith Center, Kansas, we moved back to New York City. At our parish in New York City, we have served as class parents, worked our share of carnival booths, and carpooled to track meets. We also have shared our struggles and our flaws with other parents who came from somewhere else but wanted to replicate the rhythms and values of their own school days for their kids. It has made the greatest city in the world feel like a small town for all of us. It is home.

Beyond a few hands I held of grade school crushes and my own glories on the CYO (Catholic Youth Organization) basketball courts, my memories of parochial school are sparse but indelible.

Monsignor Kearney, for one, was the first priest whom I remember laying eyes on. He was barrel-chested with a stone face and jet-black hair with brushes of gray. He always wore a cassock, sometimes with red piping, and he commanded respect or instilled fear depending on the interaction. The first time that I saw him off the altar was as a first grader during recess. He brought the kickball and hopscotch games to a halt when he strode across the playground with Rex, his massive, slobbering German shepherd that was usually at the end of a chain leash. When the monsignor was on the grounds, the pair cut a figure out of ancient Rome: the ruler with his beast. He reached into the pocket of his cassock for a roll of coins and hurled them up in the air. Then another. And another. Skittering quarters, dimes, nickels, and pennies across the blacktop igniting a free-for-all among boys in their white shirts and blue ties who bumped heads with the girls in their plaid jumpers, all of us skinning knees and elbows as we desperately dove for the bounty. When the squeals died down and he was sure all the loose change was accounted for, the monsignor held up his hand to quiet us, then bowed his head and made the sign of the cross for a blessing. With a tight, satisfied smile creasing his face, Monsignor and Rex returned to the rectory more mysterious than ever.

Two other memories that have stayed with me attest to how conservative our little corner of Midwest Catholicism really was. While I was in second grade, as *Roe v. Wade* was making it through the courts, several grades including mine were bussed downtown to what I suspect was a "Right to Life" rally. We circled the federal building with other Catholic schoolkids—stage props really—as adults chanted and prayed. The March for Life continues today, and children are still a part of it, but I do wonder how many—like me—will wonder ten or twenty or forty years from now why they were bussed to protest, a practice that they did not even understand at the time?

Finally, there was Sister Clara Marie, a young, vivacious nun who was one of the few sisters bold enough to take advantage of the more relaxed rules of the Second Vatican Council, or the shorthand Vatican II, to describe the changes that were adopted in the 1960s and shepherded by Pope John XXIII and made in the hope of making the Church more approachable to its members. Sister Clara Marie embraced Vatican II's recommendation to ditch the nun's habit and return to the order's original intention of dressing like women of the day. Still, Sister Clara Marie's street clothes did not go over well with some families. She, of course, was popular with the students. She played the piano and sang beautifully and was usually in charge of the pageants and talent shows. She caused a tremor of disapproval when she dared to have my class perform a pop song rather than a hymn. Because of her, the lyrics to the B. J. Thomas–sung, Burt Bacharach–written classic "Raindrops Keep Fallin' on My Head" is an eternal earworm that ricochets in my brain at inopportune times. Most know it from the soundtrack of the 1969 Oscar-winning film *Butch Cassidy and the Sundance Kid*. Me, I still blush at the memory of the choreography Sister Clara Marie came up with for us. Jazz-hand raindrops. Prayer hands to the side of the face for "sleeping on the job." Twirls for the helluva it. Arm sweeps for happiness.

The actual nuts and bolts of the Church's teachings of our faith was left to the Baltimore Catechism, or officially *A Catechism of Christian Doctrine, Prepared and Enjoined by Order of the Third Plenary Council of Baltimore*. It was adopted in 1855 and was based on Robert Bellarmine's 1614 *A Short Catechism*. The original version posed 421 questions to Catholic children. It was then edited down to 208 questions and has been streamlined over the centuries. It was the first and last word for Catholic schools in North America into the 1970s and is still part of the curriculum in some schools today. It was blunt, concise, and brilliant in its brevity. I'd argue that its first seven questions tell you all you need to know about Catholic doctrine.

1. Who made us?

God made us.

In the beginning, God created heaven and earth. (Genesis 1:1)

2. Who is God?

God is the Supreme Being, infinitely perfect, who made all things and keeps them in existence.

In him we live and move and have our being. (Acts 17:28)

3. Why did God make us?

God made us to show forth His goodness and to share with us His everlasting happiness in heaven.

Eye has not seen nor ear heard, nor has it entered into the heart of man, what things God has prepared for those who love him. (I Corinthians 2:9)

4. What must we do to gain the happiness of heaven?

To gain the happiness of heaven we must know, love, and serve God in this world.

Lay not up to yourselves treasures on earth; where the rust and moth consume and where thieves break through and steal. But lay up to yourselves treasures in heaven; where neither the rust nor moth doth consume, and where thieves do not break through nor steal. (Matthew 6:19–20)

5. *From whom do we learn to know, love, and serve God?*

We learn to know, love, and serve God from Jesus Christ, the Son of God, who teaches us through the Catholic Church.

I have come a light into the world that whoever believes in Me may not remain in darkness. (John 12:46)

6. *Where do we find the chief truths taught by Jesus Christ through the Catholic Church?*

We find the chief truths taught by Jesus Christ through the Catholic Church in the Apostles' Creed.

He that heareth you heareth me; and he that despiseth you despiseth me; and he that despiseth me despiseth him that sent me. (Luke 10:16)

7. *Say the Apostles' Creed.*

I believe in God, the Father Almighty, Creator of heaven and earth; and in Jesus Christ, His only Son, Our Lord; who was conceived by the Holy Ghost, born. of the Virgin Mary, suffered under Pontius Pilate, was crucified, died and was buried. He descended into hell; the third day He arose again from the dead; He ascended into heaven, sitteth at the right hand of God, the Father Almighty; from thence He shall come to judge the living and the dead. I believe in the Holy Ghost, the Holy Catholic Church, the communion of Saints, the forgiveness of sins, the resurrection of the body, and life everlasting. Amen.

So there you have the bedrock on which my faith was built. In fact, I was reminded how conservative my Catholic education was when I found the obituary of Monsignor Kearney. He died from injuries suffered in a car accident in 2003 at the age of eighty-five. Hundreds showed up at his memorial Mass despite the fact that he had not been the pastor at Christ the King since 1978 when he was removed by the bishop. Monsignor Kearney was popular with his conservative parishioners but not so much with diocesan hierarchy. He was slow to embrace the more relaxed attitude encouraged by Vatican II. There were no guitar Masses or children's choir for him. He was old-school and vowed to remain that way in the parish that he had helped build into a powerhouse of nine hundred families. The bishop at the time, John L. Sullivan, reassigned him to another parish. Monsignor Kearney refused to go. More than 150 of our parishioners held a prayer rally outside the chancery. The bishop did not budge and Monsignor Kearney was removed. Three years later, there was a noisier demonstration outside the church when the new pastor moved the tabernacle—where the Blessed Sacrament (the consecrated host) is kept—from the main altar to a side one. That ten or so feet caused a near riot. By that time Monsignor Kearney was retired, living in a big house in south Kansas City, and saying Mass there on Sundays for a large congregation of loyalists. We were not among them.

Father John Weiss, pastor of Christ the King at the time of the memorial Mass, acknowledged the large crowd and called Monsignor Kearney a "super priest," as he had been dubbed in a local paper. He ticked off his good works among the community, including opening his arms to an African American couple who had moved into the neighborhood. They converted to Catholicism on the strength of Monsignor's house call. Father Weiss also asked, "What if?"

"What impact might he have had on other parishes, other people?" he asked. "What if he had been allowed to stay? A lot of lives might have been different, including mine. But those are moot questions. Now the lives of people we know and love, filled with decisions and actions so poignant, move into history and are for a kind and compassionate God to judge. We are left with our memories and relationships."

Near the end of the obituary, a couple of facts jumped off the page at me. Monsignor Kearney was just two years older than Father Kapaun and had attended both Conception and Kenrick seminaries. They almost certainly had crossed paths. It is a small thing, I know, but alongside Father Weiss's words, it brought into focus the nagging doubts I had about this project, and about me. What was the state of my own faith? What did I believe?

Hard questions and maybe too late in the game to be asking them. Or was it?

The last time I had come to Kansas and invested in its people and stories I was in my midforties, a first-time father of a toddler. Ostensibly, I came to chronicle an undefeated, record-breaking small-town high school football team whose coach and community ascribed to an ethos of love, patience, and hard work. They won all their games by never talking about winning. Instead, they lived the motto of "Let's get a little bit better each day." Before we even moved there, I knew what I was looking for: to reconnect to my roots in the hopes of becoming a better father, husband, and person. I needed to strip myself of New York, slow down, think more of others before myself, and get a running start at navigating a young boy through the world.

Still, the meaning of my involvement with Father Kapaun was eluding me. I'm not a theologian. I always have tried to adhere to the cocktail party rule that, like sex and politics, religion is not proper conversation. If I had to sum up my personal faith, it was a gumbo of spirituality rather than a religion at the mercy of a rulebook. I can't help but to know the Mass prayers by rote because of my history. Most of the time, however, I am not exactly entranced by its rituals. I prefer drop-in church visits and lighting a candle, taking a few minutes to go wherever my mind leads. I cannot get my mind around heaven, but I believe everyone goes there if (a) they try to lead a good life and (b) they ask for forgiveness along the way and especially in their final moments. Reincarnation appeals to me. One of my favorite books, *The Power of Your Subconscious Mind* by Dr. Joseph Murphy, was given to me by my mother on my thirteenth birthday. It introduced me to the notion that if you embrace your mysteries, you can solve them or at least master them. In my interpretation, the subconscious is where God lives and where connections are made. Why can't that energy and spirit continue to exist in other consciousnesses? Okay, I'm not a shaman, either.

But the innocuous sentence about Monsignor Kearney's theological education spurred me to make some connections. Father Kapaun had led me to Father Hotze, ricocheted me back to Monsignor Kearney, and left me with a clear conclusion. Did the story of Father Kapaun stay with me for a decade and motivate me to put words about him on pages like these because I was *lacking* faith? No, not really. I believe. Was I *uncomfortable* with my faith? A bit, maybe. I was in the company of two priests—one living, one dead—and both had not only articulated what they believed but also had lived it. In the case of Father Kapaun, he believed in being Christ-like in unbearable conditions. He held the dying and broken-spirited in his arms. Father Kapaun gave hope to the hopeless. He was taunted and tortured, and even tempted with the choice of an easier way. He refused, however, to abandon his men or his faith.

I was not looking to become a priest or a saint, nor was I in despair and in desperate need of salvation. I just wanted to be closer to God and I didn't know how. After twisting myself in knots trying to pinpoint my doubts, it felt good to finally say that. Figuring out how? Well, that was going to be a path of its own, but I knew it was going to require the help of a priest.

Not any priest, but a Jesuit. If I had gone to an all-boys high school run by Benedictines or Marist priests, I am sure I would have turned to one of them. That said, I never thought every Jesuit I have ever come across hung the moon. And I did not love all of my four years at Rockhurst High School. But put eight hundred boys together and tell them you are going to challenge everything they say or do, that you will demand rigorous thinking and encourage them to question the Church and their own faith and that of the world's greatest thinkers and the whole of the Western canon, all without beating the rowdiness or rebellion out of them—then you've got a Jesuit high school. The Jesuits gave me the love of the written word and taught me how to employ it. Shakespeare, Chaucer, Mallory, and Johnson were read, studied, and dissected. The *New York Times Magazine* list of the 500 Most Underused Words in the English Language? We had daily vocabulary quizzes on them, twenty at a time. No Baltimore Catechism was taught there. Over the course of four years, we read the Bible from back to front as the sacred text it was. We broke down its origins, challenged its elements, debated about conflicting interpretations. A Man for Others meant service to each other and the community at large. Ad Majorem Dei Gloriam, or AMDG, Latin for "For the greater glory of God," is its motto and a command: We do everything for Him.

One of my mentors, Father David Bishop, once told me that if he did his job, I would have enough reasons to leave the Church but many more to come back to it.

I had a Jesuit in mind whom I hoped would nudge me in the right direction: Father James J. Martin. He was about my age and sometimes said Mass at our parish in New York. He also was a journalist and writer whose real job was editor at large for *America* magazine. He graduated from the Wharton School at the University of Pennsylvania and came to his vocation late in life after a career in business. He was a thinker and activist, especially on LGBTQ issues. Among the many books he has authored, one focused on the lives of saints who touched his life and his relationship with them.

We had only talked once by phone, for a column I was doing before the 2018 Super Bowl about whether it was moral or not to be an NFL fan knowing what we know about the lives lost and brains damaged by concussions. Father Martin prefaced his remarks by saying he was from Philadelphia and the Eagles were playing in the Super Bowl and he was heading to his sister's home to watch the game with his mother. He apologized for being as guilty as the rest of us.

I called him. We set a lunch date. After the exchange of bona fides, who-you-knows, and gossip in the media world, we said a prayer over the Indian food we were about to eat and I explained this book and the problems I felt I was having with it.

"Do you pray?" Father Martin asked.

I told him I did.

"How?"

The seventh grader in me had me squirming and tongue-tied.

"You know, Our Fathers, Hail Marys, some Acts of Contrition, the regular stuff," I said.

"What do you pray for?"

I played with my food.

"I guess gratitude and what I'm thankful for," I said.

"You don't ask him for anything?"

"No, not really."

Father Martin set his fork down.

"Now, if your son was worried about something or afraid, wouldn't you want him to tell you, so you could help him out?" he said.

"Yes."

"Well that is what God wants us to do," he said. "God wants to help us."

By then, I was feeling like the seventh grader in

religion class who had been caught looking out the window for the last forty years. There was no way it could get worse.

Or so I thought until he asked, "Have you tried praying to Father Kapaun?"

All I could think of to utter was:

"Check, please."

5

It was June 17, 1949, and Father Kapaun was finally back where he belonged—among soldiers at Fort Bliss in El Paso, Texas. He was a captain now, a promotion after a year's tour in India and Burma as World War II wound down. Instead of the crossed rifles worn by infantrymen, he wore a simple cross that marked him as a member of the Chaplain Corps. The men called him Father or Padre, but the most important thing was that they called him often. He had earned their respect in the Far East, bouncing his jeep to the front lines with a gold ciborium—a covered cup that held the Eucharist or Communion wafers. His Mass kit was always at the ready, as were the holy oils. He was there for everyone—not just the Catholics—dropping off fruit or offering a swig from his canteen. Before leaving one group of soldiers for the next, Father Kapaun bowed his head in prayer—the Catholics would recite an Our Father or a Hail Mary along with him; the non-Catholics would drop their chins and respectfully nod along. Bishop Winkelmann marveled at the monthly dispatches Father Kapaun sent—in and out of wartime—accounting for his time. He had put twenty-five hundred miles on his jeep in most months, patrolling the front lines. His Masses totaled dozens a week and attracted hundreds of soldiers. He heard as many confessions. He baptized young men, most of them frightened, and performed too many last rites on boys who were going home in a box.

But before El Paso, Bishop Winkelmann had several other missions in mind for Father Kapaun. He thought Father Kapaun had many talents to be shared throughout a wider swath and more diverse constituency of the dioceses. When Father Kapaun was released from the army at the end of the war, the bishop made sure that the young priest knew he had plans for him. The first thing that he wanted him to do was to get a master's degree from The Catholic University of America in Washington, DC. That was what the GI Bill was intended for—to give those who served a pathway to a better life. In the case of Father Kapaun, Bishop Winkelmann understood that by sending him to get a master's degree in education Father Kapaun could help lift up the young people in his growing diocese. Father Kapaun did not want to go. He was a country boy who preferred wheat fields and wooded streams to the concrete of a big city. Not only was he a priest, he also was a soldier who knew the importance of accepting orders. In Washington, DC, it did not take long for Father Kapaun to fall back into the life of the mind. He once more was an exceptional student, and he completed his dissertation. It was entitled "A Study of the Accrediting of Religion in the High Schools of the United States."

Bishop Winkelmann died before Father Kapaun earned his degree in the spring of 1948, but his replacement, Bishop Mark Carroll, agreed with his predecessor that Father Kapaun could be a dynamic contributor at home. He denied Kapaun's request to return to military service and instead assigned him to another Bohemian parish, this time in the central Kansas town of Timken. Bishop Carroll and the young priest, however, struck up a friendship, one close enough that after six months Father Kapaun wrote the bishop and asked once more to be allowed to join the army. It was what God had put him on earth to do, he told the bishop.

That is how he found himself in the desert of west Texas with the Antiaircraft Artillery Corps. It was one hundred degrees outside, but Father Kapaun was sleeping well at night in the dry air. He had not had a single day off since arriving and missed a meal or two most days. His men lined up outside his office and ducked into his room day and night. Father Kapaun marched with them. He took part in all their military maneuvers. At some point, he would ship out to Japan and join the peacekeeping forces of the 1st Cavalry Division. He could not have been happier, even though some of the men fretted about the escalating tensions in Korea. The Soviets backed North Korea and found the country vital to spreading Communism, while the United States stood firmly behind the democratic government of South Korea. The stakes were high on both sides and the prospect of another conflict had unsettled the fort.

Now, however, all he wanted to do was finish a letter to Enos and Bess. Father's Day was approaching, and even though he had started the letter several days prior, it was going to be late.

"I do feel ashamed for writing so little," he began. "Sunday is Father's Day. So I want to wish you the best of everything, Dad. I encouraged my soldiers to be sure to remember their dads on this day, and I myself did not get to write or send you something until today and I suppose you won't get this in time for Father's Day. So you see what the life of a Chaplain is, always something to be done, and done right now. But I like it very much."

On June 25, 1950, the Korean People's Army, seventy-five thousand soldiers strong, followed Soviet-made tanks across the 38th parallel, the boundary between the Soviet-backed Democratic People's Republic of Korea to the north and the pro-Western Republic of Korea to the south. The Cold War was suddenly hot. The 8th Cavalry Regiment of the 1st Cavalry Division was already in Japan, keeping the peace and training for a war against the Communists—North Korea, Russia, China—whoever showed up. As the troops prepared to go to battle in a place most of them had never heard of, Father Kapaun sensed this was going to be a different type of mission. He had entered World War II alongside battle-hardened soldiers who had the momentum to finish off the enemy. As they set sail for Korea, Father Kapaun found these soldiers were younger, greener, and not all that certain about what awaited them. Thousands of cavalrymen converged on the port city of Yokohama, Japan, to ship to Korea. Father Kapaun tried to introduce himself to as many of them as possible.

One of them, a Texan named Joe Ramirez, killed some time with the chaplain, who was a farm boy like many of them and a captain who didn't talk down to the enlisted men. When they landed in Korea, Ramirez asked Father Kapaun to baptize him. It was a good thing, because as soon as they landed, they were marched across fetid rice paddies thick with mosquitoes and up mountains in ninety-plus-degree temperatures—mortar fire landing near them the whole time. Just five days after arriving, the battalion was overrun in Kumchon, Korea, and experienced its first taste of hand-to-hand combat. The American troops were already stretched thin by the taxing and unfamiliar terrain, and the Reds, as the men called them, outnumbered them fifteen to one. The mortars had already claimed some of them, and the *rat-a-tat* of machine guns and *pops* of small arms were the soundtrack to the chaos. Father Kapaun and Dr. Jerome Dolan, an army surgeon, were dug in when one of Dolan's medics rushed in and said that his platoon leader had been wounded but had ordered his men to leave him so as not to compromise their chances to escape. Dr. Dolan got on the radio with his colonel, and two squads were redirected to extract the platoon leader and the soldiers who stayed behind with him.

Father Kapaun thought the platoon leader was too far away to make it back safely on his own. Even though two rescue squads had been dispatched, he grabbed a stretcher and, with his assistant, headed toward the wounded platoon leader as bullets hit near their feet and whizzed over their heads. No one thought they would make it back. When the rescue squads finally arrived back at command, not only was Father Kapaun with them but so was the platoon leader, as well as another wounded enlisted man no one knew was missing. Word spread about the priest-led rescue. It would eventually earn Father Kapaun a Bronze Star. Dr. Dolan meanwhile recognized the immediate and important impact that the daring rescue had on the cavalrymen. Many of these soldiers had engaged an enemy for the first time. They had survived; "No matter what mess you get into, 1st Battalion will get you out!" became their rallying cry.

The battalion got in messes daily for the next two weeks as it gained and lost ground. Father Kapaun raced from foxhole to foxhole, as the front lines were now his parish.

His helmet sat heavy past his ears; a chalice was attached to his belt. He had taken to carrying two canteens, as well as stuffing his knapsack and pockets with apples and peaches he had foraged. He would toss the canteen in first, slide in himself, and then hand over the fruit. Sometimes, Father Kapaun took a minute for some small talk and to pack his pipe with tobacco. He'd offer them a puff.

"You mind a quick prayer?" he'd ask.

No one said no. It didn't matter whether they were Catholic or not.

Joe Ramirez thought the priest was crazy. Most of the time he was afraid to put his head up, but every time he did he saw the priest bopping around the battlefield while bullets were spraying like a fire hose. A sniper bullet once buzzed close enough to cut the priest's pipe in half. His jeep and his trailer were blown up, destroying his Mass kit and clothes. Fortunately, he always kept the Eucharist and holy oils in his field jacket. His assistant was shot and sent to the hospital. Not long after, he was side by side with another chaplain, Arthur Mills, a Protestant, when a mortar landed and blew part of his colleague's leg off.

In one of the villages abandoned by rice farmers, Father Kapaun found an old bicycle. The front tire wobbled, the back tire was practically sideways, but he pedaled it from squad to squad throughout the day, dropping off the water and fruit and praying with his boys.

When the battalion claimed a hill or had run off

some Reds, Father Kapaun stacked ammo boxes and balanced a stretcher atop them for a makeshift altar just as he had as a boy for his make-believe Masses. It didn't matter that mortar fire was landing forty yards away—he shared the Eucharist and stayed to hear confessions from soldiers knowing that they were being sent out to patrols within minutes or hours. All he had to do was look at his blood-soaked uniform and keep track of the number of last rites he gave to dying soldiers to take measure of the carnage that he was in the midst of—his boys had killed thousands, he estimated. He didn't want to know how many Americans had died. Sadder still were the Korean families he passed as they fled after their villages were destroyed. Mothers were crying as they carried infants and tugged on the hands of their little ones. Behind them, their husbands and sons were pushing wagons with food and meager belongings that they managed to salvage.

Both sides were exhausted, terrified, and on edge. Father Kapaun was doing reconnaissance with a squadron when they came across a North Korean soldier in a ditch clutching a grenade. The GI's raised their guns to shoot him. Father Kapaun stepped forward and held out his canteen. He shook it and nodded, "go ahead." They stared at each other as his boys stared down the barrels of their rifles. Finally, the North Korean took the water and surrendered.

It did not take long for word of the "all man" priest to spread throughout the troops. Father Kapaun did not command anything, but he inspired loyalty, especially among the enlisted men. They watched time after time as he risked his own life to search for the wounded.

In mid-battle, Father Kapaun watched as an officer ordered an assault on a hill dotted with North Koreans, machine guns pointing down on them.

"Is this necessary?" he asked. "Isn't it kind of dangerous to attack this hill?"

The officer stood down. The North Koreans left without firing a shot.

He could be funny as well. He was sitting in a jeep one afternoon with a rifle propped up next to him. When a startled soldier asked him why he was armed, Father Kapaun smiled: "The Lord helps those who help themselves."

Eventually, the fighting subsided. The 1st Cavalry had secured a perimeter near the Nakdong River. While his men got some rest, Father Kapaun wanted to go check on some other companies in the area. He had no way to go see them. The 8th Cavalry was moving through and Father Kapaun tended to those soldiers. He asked an officer, Captain Joseph O'Connor, if he could get some transportation. O'Connor had heard of the chaplain; he told him he could have a jeep.

"No, I don't want to put you out," said Father Kapaun, winning another fan.

In mid-August, he finally had a moment to decompress. He needed to write Bishop Carroll. He apologized for the poor condition of the paper and ink that he had scavenged.

"Many thanks for your kindness and remembrances. It must be the prayers of the others which have saved me so far," he wrote.

Not wanting to alarm his friend and boss, he skipped his near-death experiences and the horrors he had witnessed. He remained upbeat, though, saying that help was on the way in terms of more soldiers and that "we should give them a good licking."

He assured the bishop that he was performing his spiritual duties, but since he had lost all his records in the jeep explosion he had to guess on the numbers: Sunday Masses drew more than two hundred soldiers. He had heard four hundred confessions, baptized two boys, and prepared another six or eight for their First Confessions and First Communions.

"War is terrible! I feel sorry for the Korean people who have to leave their homes. As the Reds approach, nearly everything is destroyed—homes, lives, and food," he wrote.

Then Father Kapaun told him what the bishop knew all along.

"I am glad to be with the soldiers in time of need."

The additional American troops Father Kapaun had prayed for arrived in a surprise attack at Inchon. The amphibious attack behind enemy lines freed up the 1st Cavalry to press on toward Seoul and lifted spirits among the soldiers. The Reds were on the run and Father Kapaun thought the war might be over within weeks. On October 1, 1950, the 1st Cavalry rolled into the village of Anseong around noon, catching its North Korean occupiers by surprise. The firefight was over quickly, and the village, about forty miles south of Seoul, was in American hands. The posters of Joseph Stalin and North Korean ruler Kim Il Sung came down. The flags of the United States and South Korea went up. Enemy soldiers replaced the locals in the village's jails and refugee camps.

Anseong was the closest Father Kapaun had been to civilization for months. He found his way to the hospital and offered to help with the village's civilian population. At first, the doctors or nurses could not understand him. He pulled out his rosary beads as well as the stole, or vestment, he wrapped around his neck when saying Mass. Finally, he pointed to the white cross on his helmet and then made the sign of the cross. They understood—a nurse took him out of the hospital and through narrow, twisting alleys until they reached the village's Catholic church. It had been trashed—the crosses were broken and the statues shattered. The altar, however, was still standing. Father Kapaun told the 1st Cavalry's interpreters to spread the word that he would conduct Mass the following morning to celebrate the liberation of Anseong.

Alongside some soldiers and villagers, Father Kapaun

cleaned up the church the best that he could. The following morning, he was joined by an overflowing local crowd eager to practice their faith in public again. They even provided two Korean altar boys who understood the Mass's cues and could recite the prayers in Latin. The Koreans could not understand the Americans and the Americans could not understand their hosts, but Father Kapaun knew that here before the altar they spoke a common language. His hosts mobbed him after Mass. They tugged at his garments and hugged him with tears in their eyes. After all the cruelty and death that he had witnessed, Father Kapaun was himself moved to tears. These people had never lost faith.

The 1st Cavalry pushed on to Seoul in good spirits, and those spirits were lifted even more now that South Korea's capital was under the control of United Nations forces. Now it was on to Pyongyang, North Korea's capital, to end the war once and for all. Before crossing the 38th parallel, the regiment stopped in Munsan, a rural town on the south bank of the Imjin River. Father Kapaun found a wheat field on the south side of town that could have been transplanted from the Great Plains of Kansas. He hung his stole around his neck and spread out an altar cloth on the hood of his jeep. He was hopeful that the end of the war was near.

"Take good care of yourselves," he told his boys as he finished Mass.

It was a good thing—there were skirmishes along the way to Pyongyang. He continued to ride along with the medics to look for the wounded. One afternoon, they were on their way back to camp with a couple of soldiers in tough shape. Suddenly, the driver was slumped next to him, wounded by machine-gun fire. Father Kapaun grabbed the wheel and somehow zigzagged between mortar explosions and bullets pinging the jeep, to get them all to safety.

His fearlessness once again was the talk of the regiment.

On October 19, 1950, members of the 1st Cavalry were on the outskirts of Pyongyang listening to the church bells ring a welcome. The boys had built a pontoon bridge over the Taedong River, and they entered the capital city gingerly. The city showed signs of war—craters, rubble, the smell of munitions. But its more than 500,000 residents were gone, mostly. Father Kapaun, who was now attached to the 8th Cavalry Regiment, was sent to the northern part of the city. Their mission was to secure the perimeter and round up any prisoners. He at least had a bed in what looked like a military academy, as well as a shower and, finally, polished combat boots. This was a luxury of civilization compared to the months he spent in the field in sweat-stained, monsoon-soaked clothes. Rations were replaced with meat and vegetables, and the comedian Bob Hope brought a USO show to town.

Father Kapaun, however, was conspicuously absent. He offered daily Masses, but he missed meals and appeared to be preoccupied. One night, Captain O'Connor saw him near a building the battalion had occupied and made as their headquarters. He followed Father Kapaun to a ramshackle hut next door, where he found him sitting on an ammunition box and hunched over a desk made from an ammo crate. He had a pen, paper, and a stack of cards—more than five hundred. On the cards were the names of the men who had been killed in combat. Each also had the name and address of next of kin, and a remark to let him know whether the soldier had been given his last rites. Father Kapaun was writing personal notes to the soldiers' loved ones, reassuring them they had died under the loving gaze of Christ. When Captain O'Connor offered to help, Father Kapaun waved him off.

"Thank you," he said, "but this is a chaplain's job."

6

It was All Saints' Day—November 1, 1950—and Father Kapaun couldn't have been busier. He had said four Masses and, in between, heard the confessions and worries of scores of soldiers. The day before, on Halloween, the battalion had dug in at Unsan, a mining town in a valley near the Nammyon River in North Korea. The cavalry had been told they were winning the war and that it might come to an end within days. But the boys were spooked by their new camp in Unsan—it looked long abandoned and it was ringed by hills whose blackness contributed to a feeling of doom. They had been battered in the previous weeks and the battalion had lost nearly half its men. Burrowed in foxholes, snow flurries dancing around them in twenty-degree weather, the men shared one common thought: this war could not be over fast enough. As darkness descended, they were unnerved even more when a string of forest fires ignited in the hills to the north and west of their position. Smoke wafted and cinders swirled amid the snow. Soon, a canopy of smoke and soot joined the descending darkness, which made it impossible for American reconnaissance planes to get a look at what was happening in those hills.

Suddenly, a chorus of bugles sounded, accompanied by the trill of whistles and bells. Thundering hooves of horses rolled in with the smoke. Rocket artillery lit up the sky and, as grenades exploded and bayonets slashed through the air, the free-floating anxiety of the boys was replaced by a sickening flesh-and-blood vision. It was the Chinese descending on them. The Chinese forces weren't supposed to be here, at least that was the intelligence that General Douglas MacArthur and the high command had shared with them. No matter its commitment to Communism and North Korea, the reasoning went, China would avoid American engagement at all cost. They were wrong—and here came twenty thousand Chinese troops. The three thousand American and South Korean soldiers that were scattered across the valley were outnumbered and woefully unprepared. There was a one-mile gap between the 1st and 2nd Battalions. The Chinese poured through.

Father Kapaun was with the 3rd Battalion in a tent on a cornfield. He was taking advantage of a rare night in the rear guard and had gone to sleep early. Before midnight, however, retreating American soldiers and swarming Chinese troops were overrunning the cornfield. Father

Kapaun and his assistant, Private Patrick J. Schuler, got in their jeep and hauled all the wounded they could fit into it, and then they loaded more wounded onto their trailer. They dropped them off at the battalion command post where what was left of the 3rd Battalion was trying to reorganize. Father Kapaun and Schuler headed back to get more fallen soldiers. But there was a roadblock. Chinese soldiers posing as South Korean forces had sneaked in behind them and had blocked all the roads.

"Stay with the jeep and say your prayers," Kapaun told Schuler.

The 1st Battalion had mostly escaped, as had part of the 2nd, but now the 3rd, the rear guard, was on the front line of a slaughter. The battlefield was so thick with soldiers that machine-gun fire gave way to hand-to-hand combat. Neither side wanted to kill one of their own. Father Kapaun, along with Dr. Clarence Anderson, dragged the wounded back to a log dugout the North Koreans had built to hide their vehicles. The officers from the retreating 1st pleaded with the chaplain and the doctor to escape with them. Neither would go. There were about two hundred soldiers left and they huddled inside a perimeter barely a couple hundred yards wide. For the soldiers too wounded to extract, Father Kapaun dug trenches to keep them out of the line of fire.

"I'm going to give you guys last rites because a lot of you guys are not going to make it home," Father Kapaun said.

He had already retrieved fifteen injured soldiers when he spied another wounded infantryman staggering outside the perimeter. Father Kapaun made a break for him.

"Stay down, Chappie, they'll shoot you, too," shouted Lieutenant Willard Lathem.

Before Father Kapaun got to the soldier, however, he was intercepted by a gaggle of Chinese soldiers.

"There goes the chaplain," screamed Lieutenant Walt Mayo.

A half dozen American rifles went off. The Chinese soldiers returned fire and for a moment forgot about Father Kapaun, allowing him enough time to escape into the darkness. At daylight, there was finally silence. The Chinese ascended into the hills. They had what was left of the Americans surrounded. In the light of day, both sides could see that the valley was scattered with hundreds of dead bodies. The Chinese would wait for the dark to mount another offensive. Still, there was a glimmer of hope when American bombers dropped ordnance and strafed the hillside loaded with Chinese troops. A helicopter to evacuate the wounded tried to land. The Chinese trained their guns on it and the rescue mission was aborted. Then a message got through: relief was on its way. Two companies of the 5th Cavalry were going to punch through the Chinese positions.

Late that afternoon, however, another message reached battalion command. The 5th was miles away and unable to get past the Chinese. It was time to evacuate.

Father Kapaun told Schuler to get out. He was going to stay with Dr. Anderson and the men too injured to escape. What was left of the 3rd held off one, two, three—in all six—charges from Chinese forces. There were about forty wounded survivors in the dugout, but their numbers were dwindling as rifle shots rained and grenades rolled into their midst. It was time to either surrender or die. Among the Americans in the dugout was a Chinese officer. Father Kapaun got through to him that they were ready to give up. In Chinese, the man shouted out for a cease-fire—the Americans wanted to surrender. Guns up, the Chinese entered and quickly hustled Father Kapaun and whoever could walk out of the log dugout. Father Kapaun appealed to their captors not to shoot the seriously wounded, but he understood the reality of what could happen.

Out of the corner of his eye, Father Kapaun saw a Chinese soldier pressing the muzzle of his rifle into the forehead of a wounded American. He broke ranks, walked straight to the soldier, and pushed him and his rifle aside. He reached down for the GI, a man named Herb Miller, a sergeant who had landed in Normandy on D-Day. His ankle had been shattered by a grenade and he had taken a bullet to his leg. These wounds, however, had not stopped him from fighting. Miller hid in this ditch all night, firing shots and tossing grenades whenever the Chinese got close to the perimeter. When he ran out of ammo and grenades, he had pulled the bodies of the Chinese soldiers he had killed on top of him to hide.

"Let me help you up," Father Kapaun said, lifting Miller onto his back.

The Chinese soldier kept his rifle trained on the pair, but he did not fire as the priest carried Miller off. They were marching north—now as prisoners of war. Of the eight hundred members of the 3rd Battalion who were in Unsan, about six hundred of them had been killed or captured. The Chinese marched the men through the snow and frozen ground only at night. No one could talk. No one knew where they were going. Miller, riding piggyback, felt Kapaun flinch every time a rifle shot went off. Both knew that one of their fellow GI's had just been killed because they were too badly wounded to keep moving.

"You should put me down," Miller said. "You can't keep this up."

"If I put you down, Herb, they'll shoot you," he said.

When the rifle shots began coming more frequently, Father Kapaun doubled back in the line, Miller still on his back, urging soldiers to pick up the more badly wounded. During the day, when they could stop, he scavenged rice sacks and branches and thread and turned them into stretchers. He never took a break. Joe Ramirez had been hit five times and was barely on his feet. But he took his turn carrying those who couldn't walk at all. How could he not?

He had watched Father Kapaun rush into one firefight after another without hesitation to pull the wounded out of further harm. He was not alone. The chaplain's example rallied his fellow soldiers to find strength they never knew they had. In one of his sermons about Jesus's triumphant return to Jerusalem on Palm Sunday, Father Kapaun foretold what was needed now.

"Men find it easy to follow one who has endeared himself to them," he said. "A man finds it a pleasure to serve one who has saved his life."

This was a death march, one that lasted for weeks and stretched out for nearly sixty miles over frozen mountain buttes. The Americans were fueled, if you can call it that, by little food. Over a mountain pass, the Chinese became impatient and loaded—poured really—some of the most seriously wounded into an American truck they had captured. They were wedged in like sardines. Father Kapaun joined them, and he folded himself into a sliver of space. The men were so broken he was afraid to move. Many were screaming in pain already. As they bumped over a ridge in below-zero temperatures, Father Kapaun led them in rosary—at first at a voice that reached a yell so it could be heard over the howling of the soldiers. The Chinese guards did not like it and banged at the truck's sides to quiet them. Soon, however, misery was replaced by a chorus, a whispering one that grew into a crescendo.

"Holy Mary, Mother of God, pray for us sinners, now and at the hour of our death, Amen."

The following morning, they arrived in Pyoktong, a city on the Yalu River. The trip ended, and it was a relief. Father Kapaun, his feet frostbitten, his legs numb, fell out of the truck and onto a rock, swelling his knee to the size of a softball. He took a look at his men, the few still ambulatory, and saw they had diminished to near skeletons, the flesh hanging off their bones. He had dropped forty pounds himself. They were herded into a huge hall and given some food, sort of—splintered kernels of corn, cabbage soup, and unsweetened sorghum, a grain fed to livestock. Next, they were led to a tangle of wooden huts near a pig farm and slammed inside at gunpoint.

Was this where they were going to die?

With a home base finally established, the Chinese were eager to interrogate the chaplain who ignored their pointed rifles, rallied the walking dead, and defied them at every turn. He hobbled into their headquarters and stood impassively as they threatened and harangued him. He just shrugged when they asked about military positions that he had no way of knowing. They tossed his field jacket and found his stole, oils, and ciborium. For some unexplained reason, they let him keep them.

After he was dismissed, without permission he went from hut to hut to check on his boys. They were stacked as many as thirty-five to a room the size of his father's woodshed. Some wanted a Rosary said, others a smile, some reassurance and a blessing.

They had been on the pig farm for just a couple of

days when they heard the reassuring rumble of a B-26 rolling over their heads. The Chinese soldiers were unnerved. They flung the doors of the huts open and fired into the air, rushing their prisoners out past the edge of town and scrambling up another hill. There were other prisoners from American units there, smoking cigarettes rolled from oak leaves and looking as tattered and hollowed out as Father Kapaun's bunch. Suddenly, the bombers' munitions set Pyoktong alight. Boom! Boom! Boom! The prisoners collapsed there on a frozen slope and watched the city burn to the ground.

That night, it was time to move again. The Americans were herded down the hill where their wounded compatriots had been left. One of them was Lieutenant Mike Dowe, who was new to the death march. He and Lieutenant William Funchess were members of the 19th Infantry and had been captured in Anju. They had already experienced brutality at the hands of their Chinese captors on their way to Pyoktong. Many of their wounded had been turned on their stomach and shot in the back of the head. When the Chinese wanted a ring off a dead soldier's hand, a knife was pulled and the whole finger was cut off. One Chinese soldier had already provided Dowe with a near-death experience. He pulled his pistol, put it to Dowe's head, and fired. The chamber was empty.

Dowe was numb when he was ordered to pick up a stretcher with a barely breathing soldier on it and march off into the darkness. He stumbled over a frozen road in the dark, the tree branch that had been fashioned into a handle threaded through the stretcher grinding into his right shoulder. When the Chinese stopped the march, Dowe and the other men rotated their positions. Dowe noticed the man holding up the back end of the stretcher. The man had thick shoulders, gray wide-set eyes, and a scraggly beard dotted with red with a tuft of goat hair on the chin. Dowe felt the strength in this man and wanted to know him.

"I'm Mike Dowe," he said

"Kapaun," the priest said, offering his hand.

"Father, I've heard of you."

He and Funchess had been asked repeatedly by captured cavalrymen if there was any word about the chaplain's whereabouts. The cavalrymen spoke reverently of how the chaplain retrieved the wounded and saved scores of lives over the course of a thirty-six-hour bloodbath.

"Don't pass it along," Father Kapaun said with a smile. "It might get back to the Chief of Chaplains."

Dowe was cheered by the wisecrack, as were the others near enough to hear it.

Soon the Chinese were yelling at them to move on.

"Let's pick them up," Father Kapaun said, instructing the soldiers who were still able to walk to pick up the wounded on the stretchers.

As far down the line as you could see, dozens of

Americans bent down, lifted, and trudged off in the dark behind the stiff-legged priest. He never gave an order. He never lost his patience. He never showed any hint of pain or despair. Father Kapaun was in charge. Like everyone else on this miserable trek, Dowe was happy to fall in line alongside him. Father Kapaun gave them hope.

He gave them comfort, too. Not long after getting back on the road, word was passed from the back of the column, soldier to soldier, that one of Father Kapaun's colleagues, Chaplain Kenneth C. Hyslop, needed his help. The Baptist minister was fading out of this world—he had been beaten so badly around the ribs and midsection that he could not eat. In fact, he had not eaten for weeks and could no longer go on. The priest stayed by the side of Hyslop as he slipped into a coma and finally stopped breathing. With the help of some soldiers, Father Kapaun clawed at the frozen Korean tundra with his hands until a grave was made. He made sure his colleague could have a proper burial.

As dawn approached, they arrived at a sprawling village in an expansive valley. It was a farming community with splintered fences and chicken coops. There were knots of round, mud-walled huts with straw roofs and clay pipes serving as chimneys for wood-burning stoves. But as the sun rose, the ramshackle buildings were eclipsed by a breathtaking vista: they were surrounded by mountains, jagged peaks with white tips that reached as high as eight thousand feet. Father Kapaun—everyone in the column—stopped and looked up in awe at the sun dancing off the mountaintops and forming a halo above them. After months of misery and bloodshed, after inhaling smoke and hearing the sound of artillery ringing in their heads every day, here, finally, was proof that God existed in this godless country.

Their Chinese captors, however, were focused on what was happening on the ground. They kicked through the doors of mud huts. They rousted the North Korean farmers and their families at gunpoint, claiming their homes as their own. The farmers wailed and cried out as they fled into the darkness, pulling their children, in some cases their grandparents, across the valley and into the woods. Soon, the valley was silent. The Chinese soldiers were as spent as their prisoners. They frantically looked for food in their new homes. They collapsed on bedrolls. The American wounded were ferried into the first huts. Father Kapaun and Dr. Anderson tried to follow them in. They were struck with gun butts and strong-armed out.

Next, Father Kapaun tried to fall in with the enlisted men. No go. His captors wanted him in separate quarters with the officers. They had recognized the sway that he held with the GI's, how they looked up to him and followed his example. He was beginning to understand the pull he had with the men as well. He saw how they relaxed in his presence and how far a simple smile went in lifting their spirits. If not the names, he knew many of the faces of the seven hundred prisoners who were now inhabitants of this valley. The ones he didn't recognize, he sought out.

"My name is Kapaun," he offered with a grin or a handshake, "glad to have you share our paradise."

Early on, the nights reached forty degrees below zero and the men slept like spoons to generate heat. There were no blankets. Their uniforms were tattered and threadbare. Some familiar faces played off the priest's energy—none more than Lieutenant Walt Mayo. He was a devout Catholic and a graduate of Boston College. He had not only fought in World War II, but he also did four months in a German prison camp. Their favorite greeting was exchanged with wry smiles and a lightning bolt of defiance.

"*Ni illegitimi carborundum esse*," Father Kapaun said.

Mayo fired back the English translation of the Latin battle cry.

"Don't let the bastards get you down."

The priest and Mayo and other brave men of the US Cavalry had already been to hell and back. They were not going to let this little patch of God's country be their burial grounds. No, this would not be Death Valley for them. Instead, they were going to make this a Happy Valley, or die trying.

1

It was Mike Dowe, the 19th Infantry lieutenant, who dubbed this hellhole in the North Korean mountains Father Kapaun's Valley. Without Father Kapaun, Dowe knew, the boys would be dropping at an unstoppable rate. From frostbite. From despair. From hunger. No matter how breathtaking their surroundings, most of the American soldiers were wounded and in miserable shape from the subzero conditions. To nourish the men's souls, Father Kapaun mixed prayers and daily kindnesses with psychology. Some of the wounded had given up, shivering and dozing off in their huts, waiting to die.

"That's Allied troops getting closer," the priest told them after hearing bombs in the distance. "We'll be out of here soon."

He knew full well that was the sound of the Chinese dropping dynamite into the nearby river to blow fish to the top so they could eat better than their prisoners. But if it got a few of them to venture out of the hut and grab a sliver of hope, then it was worth the white lie.

When a newly captured private, clearly frightened, sought out Father Kapaun for comfort, the priest employed some wry humor.

"What's going to happen to us, Father?" he asked.

"Well, they are going to shoot the officers first and let the enlisted men go," the priest said.

Another time, when a tub of food finally arrived, officers and enlisted men alike crowded around the vat with their spoons, eager to get a bite or two.

"Enlisted men first," he said to his fellow officers, "and officers eat last."

The officers stepped back and let the enlisted men's spoons scoop first.

Early in their stay, Father Kapaun had a hunch—and perhaps a divine pipeline—that their captors were eager to show that they were merciful as well as mighty by releasing some prisoners. He told a young and overwhelmed private, Peter Busatti, not to worry.

"You're going home soon," he said.

Busatti laughed. "It's okay, Father, I'm not scared, because you're around, and if I die I might get to heaven."

One night, as Thanksgiving approached, a prison guard entered the hut where the private slept and shined a light on him. He told Busatti to follow him. The private thought he might be going to his death. Then he remembered Father Kapaun's prophecy. The next day, along with two dozen wounded, he was taken to a demilitarized zone and released to South Korean and American troops. The Chinese wanted the world to know they were merciful as well as invincible.

While Father Kapaun could provide spiritual nourishment to the American soldiers, nourishing their bodies was another story. Most days, each man received 450 grams—about two cups—of cracked corn or millet, a nearly inedible cereal usually fed to livestock. It was like throwing pebbles down your throat. Clean water was hard to come by as well, and waves of dysentery were constantly rolling through the prison camp. Father Kapaun decided to become the camp's chief food thief. He told Dowe, Funchess, and Mayo of his plan, then he bowed his head and asked them to pray with him to Saint Dismas, the patron saint of those condemned to death.

So they could better understand the meaning of the prayer, Father Kapaun told them the story of the Good Thief from the Gospel of St. Luke, which is about the two criminals who were crucified alongside Jesus. The first taunted Jesus.

"Are you not the Messiah? Save yourself and us."

The other, Dismas, barked back at the criminal.

"We have been condemned justly, for the sentence we received corresponds to our crimes, but this man has done nothing criminal."

Then he said, "Jesus, remember me when you come into your kingdom."

"Amen I say to you today. You will be with me in Paradise," Jesus promised.

Then he and the prisoners all bowed their heads and prayed to Saint Dismas. Father Kapaun then stepped over the twenty American soldiers spooning on the dirt floor and slipped off into the night to scour the fields adjoining the valley. He found ears of corn and sacks of potatoes that the guards had hidden for their own meals. He grabbed as much as he could carry and brought it back to the shed. He made up to a half dozen trips that night. Soon Saint Dismas became a rallying cry for his fellow soldiers who ventured out for food. Father Kapaun was not the only good thief in the camp, but he threw his garlic, peppers, and corn into the community pile at meals for all to share. Others hoarded theirs until Father Kapaun gently admonished them with a blessing.

"Thank you, God, for the new supply of food that can be shared equally by all," he prayed. The food hoarding stopped.

His daylight heists were even more daring. The POWs prepared and ate their food together, and each day a squad of them was escorted to pick up the rations in a storage shed a couple of miles into the valley. Father Kapaun would slip in behind them and, before the squad arrived at the food depot, Dowe or Ramirez or Mayo would start a fight among themselves. While the guards tried to break up the melee, Father Kapaun would slip into the woods and raid their depot and then sneak his bounty back to camp. As often as he could, Father Kapaun took a detour to visit the enlisted men's compound. They would see him in his trademark woolen stocking cap, made from a GI sweater, lugging a one-hundred-pound sack of corn their direction. They would press to the fences for a handful, a blessing, or just a smile and a word.

Many of them were 8th Cavalry men who had been with him in Unsan. If there were no guards around, Father Kapaun made his way to the most severely wounded. He held them. He gave them Communion. He took their bloody bandages and filthy clothes to the stream that wiggled through the valley. He cracked through thick ice so he could scrub them clean. These were his boys and Father Kapaun did whatever he needed to do to keep them alive. He stole cotton T-shirts from the North Koreans. He traded his watch to the guards for a wool blanket and then cut it up and made socks for his men. With a sharp stick, he spent a whole day carving steps into a snowy slope. He wanted to make sure his boys could make it to the stream to fetch water without falling. He gave them the tobacco that he stole from or bartered for with the North Koreans. He put dried oak leaves in his own pipe and smoked that instead. All those years following Enos Kapaun around as a boy was still paying dividends. With a rock and some scrounged metal, he made pans and pots. He gathered twigs and sticks and rubbed them together to light a fire out of brush. He hung those pots and pans over an oven rack he made so the boys could have hot and clean water.

"Who wants some hot coffee?" Father Kapaun asked, plopping a smoking water pot in the middle of the room.

It was not coffee, of course, but they pretended it was each morning. They ticked off the make-believe delicacies that they would have with the coffee if they were back at home. Bagels. Scones. Toast. Donuts. Bacon and eggs. Sausage. Grits. Hash browns. Most thought they may never taste any of those again. Fantasizing, however, lifted their spirits.

Still, his guys were dying by the dozens in what everyone called the Sick House. It sure was not a hospital. There were no surgical tools or medicine, and wounds festered until they poisoned the men. Some of the sick and wounded, especially the younger soldiers, skipped meals to avoid dysentery and the vicious cycle it kicked off: painful runs in the cold to and from filthy latrines all night long. Their stomachs distended. Their wills broke. They rolled up in the fetal position and waited to die. Each morning, a few more were carried out and buried. It was a backbreaking job that no one wanted, hacking a shallow hole from frozen ground. Father Kapaun, however, was usually the first one to pick up a shovel. The priest was superhuman. It was a grim task, but Father Kapaun infused it with love and dignity.

He gently stripped the dead of their clothes, which were repurposed for the living. After the last shovel of dirt scattered on the hard ground, Father Kapaun looped his priestly stole around his neck to pray and clear the path for their rise to heaven.

"Eternal rest grant unto him, O Lord, and let perpetual light shine upon him."

When Dr. Anderson finally prevailed on the guards to let him offer what comfort he could for the sick and dying, Father Kapaun pressed to go with him.

"What these men need is medicine not prayers," a Chinese officer told him.

"Since there is no medicine, a little prayer won't hurt them," Kapaun said.

"No, you will not spread your Christian propaganda here," the officer said.

It didn't matter. Father Kapaun just got bolder in his daylight missions. He slipped into squads more often and hid behind trucks and crawled on his belly when he needed to. He knew his place was in the Sick House. He prayed over those already unconscious. He prayed with those who were soon to be unconscious. Mostly, he just held them in his arms. The rougher it got, the gentler Father Kapaun became. It didn't matter whether the person he was holding was Catholic or Baptist, Jewish or Muslim. He was there for all of them. When his visit was over, he snuck over to the enlisted men's compound.

"The Lord be with you," Father Kapaun said as he stepped into their huts.

"And with Thy Spirit," they responded like he taught them, stirring to their feet.

He started with a prayer for their comrades who had died in combat and in prison. Then he prayed for the sick and the wounded. Another prayer was for their friends and families back home. He thanked God for the favors granted them, "the food and water and wood we have from the hands of our enemy." There was a short sermon on never giving up hope, usually followed by some stern words about the enemy in the tenor of "don't let the bastards get you down."

"Be not afraid of them who kill the body," he said. "Fear him, who after he hath killed, hath the power to cast thee to Hell."

Father Kapaun was as shriveled as them, his jacket falling off his clothes-hanger shoulders, his belt cinched tight to hold up too-big pants. He smelled as bad as the rest of the prisoners of war. He hurt as much as them, too. Still, just a few minutes with him put steel in the boys' bodies and a fire to live in their hearts. Father Kapaun, somehow, brought out the good that was left in the broken bodies and spirits to a place where they could see it.

Among his inner circle, there was no less than awe for the dignity he projected. Lieutenant Dowe believed wherever Father Kapaun stood was holy ground. He swore he could turn the most fetid mud hut into a cathedral. Time after time, he watched the men gather strength from the priest's serenity and unshakable faith. Lieutenant Ralph Nardella marveled, too, at how the priest lived by God's law and how he practiced what he preached in the most brutal conditions.

How he imitated Jesus.

The guards saw it, too. In them, Father Kapaun inspired a respect bordering on fear. He was a target for the prison camp's command. They knew he was a man of God who commanded the hearts and minds of his fellow prisoners. If they could break him, if he would renounce his country and his faith, the rest of the soldiers would fall in line. They tried. They brought him in for indoctrination sessions where they would threaten and berate him. Tell him that his God had abandoned him and everyone else here. That the only way he, or anyone else, was going to leave was if they bowed to Chairman Mao and the Communist way of life. They told him that the enlisted men no longer wanted to see him. He knew better. Sometimes they roughed him up. Other times, he was stripped of his clothes and forced to stand outside in the cold, or he was relieved of his threadbare socks and shoes and made to stand on the frozen river for hours.

Father Kapaun, however, never wavered. His face was always just as placid as it was when he was a boy in Kansas, milking a cow in the sunset all by himself. He did not argue. He endured these sessions in silence, his steel-gray eyes staring right through them. They could not intimidate him.

He wore his stole and carried his ciborium and strode the camps like he was back at Fort Bliss. Religious displays were banned in the camp. The chaplain didn't care. The guards, taking note of his lack of fear, watched as he ducked from one group to another conducting services.

"There is no use risking your life in this manner," a Chinese officer told him after breaking up a service. "Prayers won't help these men."

Father Kapaun knew better than that. The captors could deprive him and his boys of food and water. They could strip them of their clothes. They could taunt and torture them. But prayer was a weapon that they could not disarm.

On Christmas, Father Kapaun gathered the officers for a service. He looked them up and down—they were a battered bunch. The quarters where they had gathered looked even worse. He told them never to despair, to only look forward. He likened their current state to Joseph and a pregnant Mary with nowhere but a ramshackle manger to stay. Look at the joy and glory that came from that night. We will get out of here and great things await us.

A couple days later, the Chinese officers running the prison believed they had just the thing to break this defiant priest and his determined followers. They brought in a troupe of North Korean children who had gone through Communist indoctrination and now were proponents of all things Mao. They were all dressed in uniforms of gray. Their angelic faces were restrained by grim-faced discipline. On cue, they sang songs to the Great Leader. One read an ode to the hammer and sickle. They performed long, choreographed dances like the ones done by peasant farmers on the mainland to ensure a successful harvest for the greater good of the people. It was a master class on how to bend the will of the people. It was turning into a long night and the prisoners were getting angry at how the Reds had drained all the joy out of these innocent children.

Mercifully, there was a short break. From the back of the audience, a GI started to hum a familiar tune. A few more chimed in with their voices.

"Silent night, holy night."

Softly, self-consciously at first, they were joined by a few more.

"All is calm, all is bright."

Father Kapaun and the officers raised their voices.

"'Round yon virgin mother and child."

Then the high-pitched voices of children offered treble to the melody. Up front, the Korean children were singing along. For the first time all night, they did not look like robots. Smiles creased their faces and made them truly angelic.

"Holy infant, so tender and mild."

The men now were singing full throated, some with

8

In mid-January 1951, Father Kapaun and his men were herded from the valley and plowed through snow-buried mountain passes back to Pyoktong, which had been reduced to rubble by Allied bombers. It was the dead of winter in the mountains of Korea, and the prisoners were ill-prepared to hike through subzero temperatures. No one had a proper coat. The guards had taken everything they possessed that would make their own lives better. The only prisoners with boots had them because the guards deemed them too tattered to be of any good. Most of the GI's had fabricated a sort of sneaker, which was made of melted rubber and cardboard. These sneakers offered little warmth for toes that were black and flaking from frostbite. Nine of the men could not go on and were left for dead after the guards refused to let the doctors or Father Kapaun attend to them.

When the prisoners finally arrived in Pyoktong, they found a waterfront town that was as wrecked as they were. There were skeletons of pagodas and piles of wood that were once schools and churches. It smelled of mortar, disease, and death.

Carved out of a corner were the remnants of thirty buildings that were ringed by barbwire and stone-faced sentinels. It had a name—Camp No. 5—and a Chinese commander named Comrade Sun whose job was to break these men down and rebuild them as Communists. Good luck with that, Father Kapaun thought, when Comrade Sun met with the officers and told him that they could either accept the mission that he offered or die resisting. Soon after they arrived, the officers were once more separated from the enlisted men, but Comrade Sun went even further. Sergeants were culled and isolated from the enlisted. Blacks and Latinos were segregated from the whites. The sick and wounded? They were carted off to an isolated patch of camp from which few would ever return.

Father Kapaun rallied his boys the best he could— they fanned out to salvage tin and nails and wood and bricks. They patched up roofs and shored up walls. In a bombed-out church, fittingly, he found everything he needed to build an outdoor fireplace where the men could cook any food they scavenged as well as gather around and stay warm. His clandestine food raids were renewed, and he set up shop to build more pans and buckets. His predawn, pretend-coffee break-fasts now extended into dinner: ten-course meals were imagined and relished—pâté and fillet, escargot and pizza, tacos and devil's food cake, fried chicken and biscuits—foods that reflected the diverse makeup of this crowded camp.

Father Kapaun made his rounds each day with a dented bucket at his side. It came in handy sometimes, but really it was his passport to move freely and get some time with as many men as possible. He thought it made him look like he was working, which lulled the guards into disinterest. As days turned into weeks, how-ever, these excursions turned into horrifying field trips of defeat and despair.

He saw firsthand the deteriorating condition of his boys. Toes and fingers fell off from frostbite. Bones poked through the skin, inflicting agony. He took them to the doctors and held them while bones were sawed off or limbs were amputated with a butcher knife that they hid from the guards. The skin of some GI's was so inflamed from lack of vitamins that it turned flame red. Many suffered from dementia. All were telltale signs of malnutrition. There was not a man, including himself, who was not covered with lice. They multiplied over-night and could become thick enough to bleed a man to death in a day. Worse, prisoners tired of picking them off, tired of living at all, and let the lice take them to eternity.

Father Kapaun tried to slow the dying. He spent hours picking lice off his boys.

"I got ninety," he called out.

"Seventy-five over here," Nardella answered.

"Cracked one hundred," someone else would sing out.

Others killed themselves by abandoning the huts and the body warmth of fellow soldiers for the outside. They went to sleep to never wake up. Then their hut mates retrieved their dead bodies and slept next to them for a few days to collect extra rations. Dead bodies were stacking up outside because the ground was too frozen to bury them. Father Kapaun carried his bucket from hut to hut and huddled with the men, willing them to stay alive.

"Don't let your families down," he said. "Whatever you do, don't stop eating."

The Chinese did not care about the health of their captives. Comrade Sun, instead, focused on his mission. He was a small, short-tempered man who desperately wanted to turn American prisoners into flesh-and-blood propaganda puppets if not red-blooded Communists. For hours, he made them sit through lessons on Lenin and Marx and memorize and recite Communist doctrines. When a prisoner refused, he was stripped of his clothes and hauled off to a hole dug in the frozen ground and sealed into solitary confinement—sometimes for days, sometimes for weeks.

Comrade Sun was quick to identify Father Kapaun as the officer with the most influence in the camp even though the priest did not hold the highest rank. He and his guards targeted him for more abuse and tried to humiliate him at every turn. Red-faced, spit flying, Comrade Sun would get in Father Kapaun's face and accuse him of spreading rumors about the Chinese.

"No, it is not anti-Communist propaganda, it is Christian love, and I shall pray for your soul," the priest said.

"Don't ask God for your daily bread," Comrade Sun said. "Ask Mao Tse-tung. He's the one who provides your daily bread. You cannot hear or see your God. Therefore God does not exist."

Father Kapaun remained stone-faced.

"One day, the Good Lord will save the Chinese and free them from the scourge that has set upon them," he said. "The Good Lord, as He fed the thousands on the mountain, will also take care of us. Mao Tse-tung could not make a tree or a flower or stop the thunder and lightning."

When Comrade Sun had the guards take away his rosary, he twisted another one from barbwire. When Comrade Sun had him stripped and sent outside to stand in the cold, he did not complain. In fact, upon his return to the officers' hut, he drew some smiles.

"When our Lord told us to love our enemies, I'm sure he did not have Comrade Sun in mind," he said.

Comrade Sun picked out two American officers, friends of Father Kapaun, for interrogation. He hung them from ropes until their wrist joints pulled apart, until they finally told him what he wanted to hear: that Father Kapaun was leading a Communist resistance and had threatened that any American who cooperated with the enemy would be court-martialed.

No one in Camp No. 5 believed the accusations, and, when the brutalized officers returned to their hut, Father Kapaun was the first to put his arms around them. He gently stroked their twisted hands.

"You never should have suffered for a moment to try to protect me," he said.

Father Kapaun wore an oversized overcoat with deep pockets so he could transport whatever he stole or foraged—garlic and rice, pepper or roots, tin or glass. Nothing went to waste. He wore an eye patch as well after catching a chunk of wood in his eye on one of his salvage missions. With his long and stringy reddish-brown hair and scraggly beard, Father Kapaun was starting to look like Jesus—or at least that is what his boys told him. It embarrassed him, but if it lifted them just a little, he decided he could live with it.

One afternoon, Mike Dowe came across Father Kapaun at rest—or the closest thing to it for the priest. He was standing by the barbwire with a hint of a smile on his face.

"What are you thinking of Father?" he asked.

"Of that happy day when the first American rolls down that road," he said. "Then I'm going to catch that little so-and-so Comrade Sun and kick his butt right over the compound fence."

It was March 25, 1951—Easter Sunday—and Father Kapaun sensed his men needed a boost. He was going to hold services—something the Chinese had not allowed. He did not ask them for permission, either. He spread the word among the officers and, at sunrise on a gray spring day still cold enough that ice clusters bobbed down the Yalu River, nearly eighty of them shuffled to a courtyard of a bombed-out church. Father Kapaun, purple stole around his neck, stood on the steps and held a small crucifix he had made by binding two sticks together. He lifted it over his head with one hand and leaned into a walking stick with the other. He was as battered and as lice-ridden as the gaunt, hollow-eyed congregation before him. There were Protestants and Jews, Muslims and atheists, British and Turkish soldiers. The Chinese guards ringed the perimeter, unsure of what was about to take place.

As Father Kapaun began to speak, he faltered. Then tears streaked beneath his eyes. His Mass kit had been confiscated at his capture. He had no liturgy. He had no Communion hosts. Lieutenant Nardella appeared at his side and handed him a missal, or book of prayers. Father Kapaun found the page that he wanted. He began reciting the Stations of the Cross, the story of Jesus's sentence to death, his torture, and finally his death on the cross. The priest knew his audience. These men had suffered gravely at the hands of their captors. They wept as they listened to the misery of the final hours of Jesus Christ. When he was finished, Father Kapaun held up the rosary that he wrought from barbwire. He asked the non-Catholics to allow him to lead them through a rosary and the five glorious mysteries. How Jesus rose from the dead. How He ascended into heaven. How He sent the Holy Spirit down so all would have the wisdom to know the truth and share it with others. How Mary, his mother, was assumed into heaven. How she was coronated in heaven and could intercede on their behalf. By the rosary's conclusion, the prisoners were saying Hail Marys regardless of their faith.

The sun was cresting the hills and, looking out to his audience, Father Kapaun knew his men were spent. He asked Bill Whiteside, an officer known for his beautiful voice, to close out the services. Whiteside belted out "The Lord's Prayer." His voice was crisp and lilting, and soon others found their voice and joined him. Loudly, so the enlisted men in the corners of the camp who were not allowed to attend the service could hear them as well.

Dr. Esensten, a Jewish doctor, got goose bumps as he looked at his fellow officers and saw joy on their faces. They were lifted by the music. They felt the solemnity, the hope, of the moment. They all felt closer to home than they had in many months.

When Dr. Esensten looked up on the stairs to the

priest, however, he also recognized something else: his friend was ailing. Father Kapaun had been hobbling along on a walking stick for weeks now, a condition he laughed off as a sign of old age. He was malnourished and hurting badly. His bones ached and his color was pallid. After all those months of taking care of everyone else, the priest had neglected his own basic needs.

On the Sunday after Easter, it caught up with Father Kapaun. When it was time for his sermon, he had trouble summoning his words.

"And this is the victory that overcomes the world— our faith," he finally mustered, then collapsed in front of the men.

When Dr. Esensten finally examined him, he peeked under his pants leg and saw that one of his legs was black-and-blue. When he touched it, Father Kapaun winced.

"One leg is twice the size of the other," Dr. Esensten said.

"How long do I have?" Father Kapaun asked.

"Two weeks."

The doctor was angry as well as frightened. Father Kapaun had a blood clot in the vein of his lower leg. It could be fatal in the healthiest of men, and it might as well have been a death sentence for someone as sick and malnourished as the priest. Dr. Esensten and Dr. Anderson decided it might be best to amputate. Father Kapaun's condition was too severe for them to amputate with a dull butcher knife. So they asked Comrade Sun to allow the Chinese doctors to perform surgery. He refused the request.

"Let God save him. He was a man of God," he said.

The doctors had no other choice but to order bed rest. Father Kapaun fought it. His fellow prisoners did not have to be asked to help the priest, after months of him doing unto others. Lieutenant Funchess, a farmer's son as well, cleared a space next to the wall where Father Kapaun would not be jostled. It had been serving as the lieutenant's recovery place, too: his right foot had been ripped through with bullets and shrapnel. Funchess slept next to Father Kapaun and held him at night to keep him warm. He heard the priest's cries at night, felt the spasms and shudders that accompany hunger.

On one of those nights, Funchess confided in Father Kapaun his fear that, at twenty-four, he was living out his final days in this miserable prison camp.

"I don't think I'm going to make it, Father," he said. "I can hardly walk on my foot. It's going to get an infection. I'm starving."

"No, no," he said, "you're going to get better. You're going to get better. So you just walk on that foot."

Then Funchess asked about forgiveness. How could they be expected to forgive their North Korean and Chinese captors who shot prisoners? How could they turn the other cheek to abuses? How could they be expected to forget these months of being treated like animals?

"Of course, we should forgive them," Father Kapaun said. "We should not only forgive our enemies but love them, too. If we fail to forgive, we are rejecting our own faith."

The whole camp was invested in the recovery of Father Kapaun. The men built a trapeze so the priest could keep the leg elevated. They heated up bricks from the church and held them against the swollen leg. They took turns carrying him to the latrines. When that became too painful for him, they fabricated a commode from a potbellied stove and one of the priest's pans. They gave him the aspirins that they had been saving for a future bout of pain. They stole food and offered up their own rations in a desperate effort to get the priest healthy. They streamed into the hut to ask for Father Kapaun's blessing or to just offer a word of help and thanks.

When dysentery compounded the priest's condition, Dr. Esensten came up with a scheme that sent dozens of men to the Chinese doctors complaining of diarrhea. The medicine that they received was repurposed for Father Kapaun. His condition seemed to improve. He could sit up from the floor and stand with the help of his boys. He was weak, but he was lucid enough to dictate to Lieutenant Funchess how to properly bend and crimp his signature buckets and water pans.

By May, most of the prisoners thought that they had successfully kept the priest from the Death House, a

Buddhist monastery on the hill above them where the prisoners in the worst conditions were sent to die. Father Kapaun knew better.

"I am going to die," he said, startling Felix McCool, who had asked Father Kapaun to hear his confession.

Father Kapaun bolted upright and blessed McCool in Latin. He had a fever and was delirious—pneumonia was settling in. He spoke to Enos and Bessie and told stories of growing up in Pilsen. Soon, Mike Dowe and Walt Mayo and Ralph Nardella and William Funchess were in the hut. They had heard about the sharp deterioration of the priest's health. Father Kapaun was crying, but he assured them that he was glad that he was suffering. Jesus had suffered, too. Now he felt closer to Jesus. Everyone who had gathered around him was in tears— they had lost friends and watched bodies pile up over the months, but the numbness left them as they witnessed his suffering. All were relieved when Father Kapaun finally fell asleep.

The following day, Comrade Sun burst into the hut with a handful of armed guards and a stretcher. He shot his gun into the air. Then he pointed at the priest.

"He goes," Comrade Sun said.

"No, he stays with us," said Funchess.

"Leave him," said Nardella.

"Leave him," cried others, crowding the guards.

The doctors, Esensten and Anderson, pleaded with Comrade Sun to leave the priest alone. He was recovering.

They would get him better. That is exactly what Comrade Sun was afraid of.

"We'll take care of him," Comrade Sun said. "He'll do better with us."

Soon, men were gathering outside the hut, pushing their way in. They were like ghosts—emaciated and moving in slow motion. They started shoving the guards. The guards shoved back with their rifles. They were scared and about to take aim.

"I'll go," came a whisper.

"I'll go," Father Kapaun repeated a little louder. "Don't get in any trouble over me."

He handed his gold ciborium over to Mayo.

"Tell them I died a happy death," he said.

He found his voice and told a story from the Old Testament book of Maccabees about how a king threatened to kill a mother and her seven sons unless they all swore off God. She encouraged her boys to "Keep the faith" and watched each of her boys tortured and killed. Then she was killed.

Father Kapaun nodded to Nardella and handed him the missal: "You know the prayers, Ralph. Keep holding the services. Don't let them make you stop."

Phil Peterson touched the priest on the arm: "I'm terribly sorry."

"You're sorry for me," he said. "I am going to be with Jesus Christ. And that is what I have worked for all my life. And you're sorry for me? You should be happy for me."

The priest singled out another prisoner.

"When you get back to Jersey, you get that marriage straightened out. Or I'll come down from heaven and kick you in the ass."

Dowe was sobbing.

"Don't take it hard, Mike," said Father Kapaun. "I'm going where I always wanted to go. And when I get there, I'll say a prayer for all of you."

Nardella and Bob Wood, who was captured with Father Kapaun at Unsan, put the priest on the stretcher as their fellow prisoners snapped to attention and formed an honor guard. Dr. Anderson looked the priest over once more. He knew how much pain he was in. He watched as Father Kapaun smiled and waved at his men from the stretcher. As the priest passed, tears streaked down the prisoners' faces.

"To Allah who is my God, I will say a prayer for you," said Fezi Bey, a Muslim soldier from Turkey.

When Nardella and Wood reached the Death House, they watched as Father Kapaun made the sign of the cross and blessed the guards. Then the priest looked at the Chinese officers awaiting his arrival.

"Forgive them," he said, echoing Jesus's words on the cross. "For they know not what they do."

He then looked the officer in charge in the eye.

"Forgive me?" Father Kapaun asked of the officer.

(Left) Emil Kapaun as a boy with his brother Eugene and *(below)* the modest home they grew up in during the Depression on the plains of Kansas.

(Left) Emil made his First Communion on May 29, 1924, at St. John Nepomucene Parish in Pilsen, Kansas *(below)*.

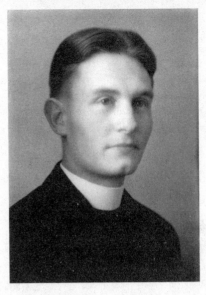

Father Kapaun as a twenty-four-year-old seminarian at Kenrick Theological Seminary in St. Louis, Missouri. He was ordained a priest months later on June 9, 1940.

While serving as pastor at St. John Nepomucene, Father Kapaun was appointed the auxiliary chaplain at the army air base in Herington, Kansas, and found his calling. In 1944, he became a full-time military chaplain.

Father Kapaun repairing the wobbly wheeled bike that he rode from foxhole to foxhole to minister to his men.

On August 11, 1950, near Taegu, Korea, Father Kapaun said Mass, as he often did, from the hood of his Jeep.

Father Kapaun with his ever-present pipe, which frequently took shrapnel on the battlefield.

(Above) Father Kapaun was known for his derring-do rescuing wounded soldiers on the battlefield. He also made it a point to write to the families of every single soldier who died in combat (left).

Father Kapaun in his trade-mark garrison hat that he wore on his rounds in Camp No. 5, a brutal prison in the waterfront town of Pyoktong. He died there at the age of thirty-five.

Some former prisoners of war cradle the crucifix made by Captain Gerald Fink, a Jewish marine pilot, to commemorate Father Kapaun. While a prisoner, Fink made the forty-seven- by twenty-seven-inch cross out of cherry wood. He bent radio wire for a crown of thorns and put it atop a twenty-six-inch Christ figure carved out of scrub oak.

Chase Kear left the Wesley Rehabilitation Hospital with his father Paul Kear and friend Mick Hanson in 2008, seven weeks after a pole vault accident that doctors believed he could not survive.

Avery Gerleman was twelve when she was stricken with an autoimmune disease that doctors told her parents she would not survive. But prayers to Father Kapaun by her family and friends inexplicably pulled her through. Eight years later, in 2014, she earned a scholarship to play soccer at Hutchinson Community College.

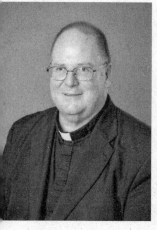

(*Left*) Father John Hotze, a Kansan, grew up praying to Father Kapaun and spent more than a dozen years amassing more than eight thousand pages of interviews and documents that showed the chaplain led a life of heroic virtue. He handed it over to Dr. Andrea Ambrosi (*below*), a canon lawyer in Rome, who wrote the *positio*—or case for the chaplain's sainthood—and is guiding Father Kapaun's cause through the Vatican.

Chase Kear at Father Kapaun's home church St. John Nepomucene in the summer of 2019. Friends, family, and strangers from across the globe prayed to the priest for Chase's recovery. They believe it was a miracle.

Avery's eighty-seven days in the hospital inspired her to become a pediatric nurse. Avery *(far right)* with colleagues Marcia Hendricks and Tammy Patterson at Newman Regional Health Medical Partners Family Medicine in Emporia, Kansas.

9

On May 23, 1951, two days after entering the Death House, the news that his fellow prisoners dreaded but expected spread through Camp No. 5: Father Kapaun was dead. No one saw his body—it was dragged across the Yalu River and dumped in a mass grave that, by war's end, was the resting place of the remains of about sixteen hundred of his fellow prisoners of war.

In the officers' hut, Lieutenant Mayo, Father Kapaun's sometime altar boy, hid the priest's gold ciborium from the guards. Lieutenant Funchess, the man who gave Father Kapaun his spot by the wall and kept him warm at night, read the Twenty-Third Psalm aloud to the men. It was a fitting eulogy for the priest who had taught them to have faith and never give up.

The Lord is my shepherd; I shall not want.

He maketh me to lie down in green pastures: he leadeth me beside the still waters.

He restoreth my soul: he leadeth me in the paths of righteousness for his name's sake.

Yea, though I walk through the valley of the shadow of death, I will fear no evil: for thou art with me; thy rod and thy staff they comfort me.

In another hut, Nardella led the men in a rosary.

In another room in the Death House, Corporal Robert McGreevy dug his hands into the dirt floor and pushed himself to his feet. McGreevy was a Marylander, a former high school football star, and just nineteen years old. He had been captured at the Battle of Unsan. He had been in the Death House for weeks and was resigned to dying there when he heard of Father Kapaun's fate. They were friends from the priest's frequent visits to the enlisted men's huts. Father Kapaun's prayers and kind words were about all McGreevy knew about hope in this hellhole. He was Catholic and knew about how saints took their place in heaven and how praying to them could lead to good things. McGreevy stood for the first time in days. He breathed deep and leaned against the wall.

"Father Kapaun, help me," he prayed.

In Pilsen, Kansas, however, closure for Enos and Bessie Kapaun was slow in coming.

On Thanksgiving Day, 1950, Father Joseph Goracy, the pastor of St. John Nepomucene, asked the couple to meet him in the rectory after noon Mass. Earlier that morning, the postman had dropped off a US Army telegram at the church. The telegram was sealed, but the postman knew the Kapauns, and he knew not only where they would be but how they might want to hear potentially devastating news. Enos, now seventy and stooped from a lifetime of farmwork, was nervous. Bessie's ever-present smile disappeared when Father Goracy told them about the telegram. She asked Father Goracy to read them the letter.

"The secretary of the Army has asked me to express his deep regret that your son, Captain Emil J. Kapaun, has been missing in action since Nov. 2nd '50," wrote Edward F. Withell, adjutant general of the US Army. "Upon receipt of further information in this office you will be advised immediately."

The couple's tears were silent and restrained. When Father Goracy offered them his prayers and all the words of hope that he could muster, Bessie accepted them eagerly. Enos did not.

"I will not see my son again on this earth," he said. "I have to wait until I get to heaven."

Eleven months later, however, an ember of hope flared for Enos and Bessie when they received a letter from Sergeant Samuel Cleckner. He had been captured with Father Kapaun and shared quarters with the priest in the valley as well as Camp No. 5. Cleckner was among the handful of prisoners released in an exchange shortly after the Battle of Unsan. He had promised to write the priest's parents and was among the first to tell newspaper reporters about their son's heroism on the battlefield and in the prison camps.

"May I say that your son is one of the bravest men I have ever met. He showed great courage and devotion to his country and faith under the most hazardous of conditions," he wrote in a letter dated October 6, 1951. "I have seen him stand unflinchingly in the face of fire in order to bring comfort and aid to some soldiers that had been wounded or to deliver the last rites in some instances. He kept up the morale of those that had been taken prisoner by his kindness and words of hope and faith.

"I sincerely wish that the Chinese would have released your son at the same time I was, and hope that you receive even more glad and important news than I can give you."

Every day thereafter, Enos and Bessie walked to the mailbox on the dirt road at their farm in the hope of getting a letter from their son or a letter from another prisoner or, God forbid, a word of their son's fate from the army. On October 18, 1952, still uncertain whether the chaplain was dead or alive in a prison camp, the army decided to hold an award ceremony to present the Kapauns the Distinguished Service Cross and Bronze Star their son had earned on the battlefield. It was held at St. John

Nepomucene in Pilsen, and the church was more crowded than it was for Father Kapaun's first Mass as a priest. Enos and Bessie received the medals graciously. But they refused to keep them. Instead, they handed them over to Bishop Carroll. They had given their son to the Church, they told him, and it should keep his medals, too.

Shortly before the war ended on July 27, 1953, Enos and Betsy received a letter from the US Army confirming their son's death. Major General William E. Bergin wrote: "I sincerely regret that this message must carry so much sorrow into your home, and I hope that in time you may find sustaining comfort in knowing that he served his country honorably. My deepest sympathy is extended to you in your bereavement."

Weeks later, when prisoners of war were exchanged, Enos and Bessie finally truly understood the impact their son had on a group of men who essentially had been left for dead and crushed of all hope. The stories about Father Kapaun, a Catholic chaplain, brought a faraway war (and a largely forgotten one now) home to a nation busy creating the American Dream. The stories were told to hungry newspaper reporters and war correspondents by diminished but hardly broken prisoners from Camp No. 5 who wanted the world to know about the hero, patriot, and leader they had lost.

"Father Kapaun's courage has the softness of velvet and the strength of iron," was the epithet Mayo chose for his friend.

Dr. Esensten and Dr. Anderson were among the priest's closest friends, and they were struck by the humility Father Kapaun embodied and the common ground that he sought for all. The Jewish doctor, Esensten, said the two rarely spoke about religion and instead encouraged each other's faith.

"I am a Jew, but I feel deeply the greatness of the man, regardless of religion," Esensten said.

Anderson remained as puzzled as he was impressed by the priest.

"More than a human being, a hero, or a saint—Father Kapaun was first an enigma, as all simple men are," he said. "You wondered why he did some of the things he did. He was a man without personal motives, without any personal regard for his safety or comfort. He simply did what his moral and ethical code told him was his duty."

Why? Lieutenant William "Moose" McClain had a theory based on a conversation he'd had with Father Kapaun about how the desperate situation they were enduring would bring out the best and worst in each of them. McClain thought Father Kapaun believed he was there to help the "best" prevail in all. For Captain Robert Burke, it was the battle that Father Kapaun waged on Burke's behalf and that of his fellow prisoners that cost the priest his life.

"Every man is proud to say, 'I knew Father Kapaun—he saved my life, he made me fight to stay alive when dying was so simple'; it was easier to die than live in those days," Burke said. "Death was a welcome relief. We owe our present happiness to that heroic man who gave his all, who sacrificed himself for his fellow man, who worked himself to death."

But perhaps the most powerful testament to the priest's unfailing courage and healing powers came from a Jewish marine fighter pilot who had never even met Father Kapaun. Captain Gerald Fink was captured and arrived at Camp No. 5 weeks after the priest had died. But Father Kapaun was very much alive among the men of that miserable place. The stories he heard about the iron-willed priest were impressive, but more inspiring was the regard his new friends had for Father Kapaun and the hope and defiance that he left behind in them. And in him. Fink decided to create a memorial to the priest, and he did so by channeling the skills that had been demonstrated by Father Kapaun—resourcefulness and ingenuity.

Fink made a chisel out of a drainpipe, and a mallet and knife out of the steel arch of a boot. He smashed a window for its glass shards to do detailed carving. Over nearly three months, he hacked a forty-seven-by-twenty-seven-inch cross out of cherry wood. He bent radio wire for a crown of thorns and put it atop a twenty-six-inch Christ figure carved out of scrub oak. The figure bore an uncanny resemblance to a man he never met: Father Kapaun. These labors earned Fink time in the hole, but the

Chinese guards did not dare take—or even touch—that crucifix. They still were afraid of the man it represented; the man they had sent to death.

On the day the prisoners were released, North Korean guards tried to take the crucifix from Fink as well as Father Kapaun's gold ciborium from Nardella. Both refused. When the men of Camp No. 5 marched out of their imprisonment, it was Fink and his crucifix that led the procession.

"If the meek shall inherit the earth, it will be because people like Father Kapaun willed it to them. I am a Jew, but that man will always live in my heart," Fink told reporters years later. "Father Kapaun not only served Christians well but he served everyone else with equal goodness and kindness. Never thinking of himself, he was always doing something for others. He represented to me saintliness in its purest form and manliness in its rarest form."

10

Valor or virtue, which means more? I put that question to Father Hotze one afternoon during a conversation at the Diocese of Wichita. We were sitting in a basement conference room where documents about all things Father Kapaun were strewn across a conference table along with an industrial-size doorstop of a bound copy of the materials that he had shipped to Rome.

For a self-described, easily distracted slacker, the priest had worn many hats in his pursuit of Father Kapaun's cause for sainthood. Skeptic. Detective. Journalist. Administrator. Champion. To me, the most important role Father Hotze plays—now twenty years since he first started this pursuit—is thinker and scholar. He is *the* Father Kapaun expert. He has felt the dirt of Pilsen, Kansas, beneath his feet. He knows its rural rhythms, its core values, and people like the Kapauns who had instilled them in the region.

He has comforted the Korean POWs who poured out their hearts and souls, terrors and tears, about their horrifying experiences. He has sat silently by their sides when they cried. He has prayed with them and for them. Father Hotze has parsed the letters and homilies of Father Kapaun. He has prayed with the young people and their families who all believe Father Kapaun interceded on their behalf to perform a miracle and return them to their health. He has spoken to their doctors to see if there was a medical reason for their recovery.

In short, there is not another human being alive who has thought more about the meaning of the life of Father Kapaun than Father Hotze.

One of the by-products of the priest's work was that on April 11, 2013, President Barack Obama awarded Father Kapaun the Medal of Honor. In the East Room of the White House for the presentation were Herb Miller, Bob Wood, Robert McGreevy, and Mike Dowe. It was Dowe who had pushed for his friend to receive the nation's highest military honor. Dowe started this effort from the moment he was released from the prisoner-of-war camp, and he never stopped putting his and his fellow prisoners' testimony about Father Kapaun front and center. As a graduate of the United States Military Academy at West Point, together with his subsequent work as a nuclear physicist, Dowe knew people in the military and defense world who could help in the cause.

They had come close to securing this honor before 2013, but it was not until the work done by Father Hotze started to get wider public notice that it came to the attention of Kansas's congressional delegation. Among them was another West Point graduate, US representative Mike Pompeo, who would become the head of the Central Intelligence Agency and the Secretary of State under President Donald J. Trump.

It also didn't hurt that President Obama's maternal grandparents were Kansans, a fact that he acknowledged in his remarks. "Now, I obviously never met Father Kapaun. But I have a sense of the man he was," the president said.

"Emil and my grandfather were both born in Kansas, about the same time; both raised in small towns outside Wichita. They were part of that Greatest Generation—surviving the Depression, joining the army, serving in World War II. They embodied those heartland values of honesty and hard work, decency and humility—quiet heroes determined to do their part."

Obama, known for his composure and oratory, was clearly moved by the story of Father Kapaun and what the priest's sacrifices meant to his comrades as well as the American character. He told of the priest's heroics starting with how he first saved, then carried, Miller for days on end. He acknowledged Father Kapaun's fellow prisoners who were in the East Room—nine in all, each pushing their nineties—and led the crowd in a standing ovation for them. By the time Ray Kapaun accepted the medal on behalf of his uncle, there was not a dry eye in the room.

"This is the valor we honor today," President Obama said. "An American soldier who didn't fire a gun, but who wielded the mightiest weapon of all, a love for his brothers so pure that he was willing to die so that they might live."

So, valor or virtue, Father Hotze?

He was clearly ready for the question and eased into an explanation that demonstrated how deeply he has internalized Father Kapaun and his teachings. He should have been at a lectern giving a homily at High Mass on Easter Sunday. He was as easy a storyteller as he was a rigorous thinker. He kicked off his lesson by citing a conversation that he had had with Phil O'Brien from the Department of Defense, for the POW-MIA section. It was O'Brien's job to identify the prisoners of war who had either died and were buried in the mass graves surrounding Camp No. 5 or who were missing in action. He had been able to identify fourteen hundred, but another two hundred went unidentified and were likely to remain so because there were not many Korean War veterans left.

It was a different kind of detective work—grimmer for certain—but it bonded O'Brien to Father Hotze, and they helped each other out whenever they could. O'Brien was not Catholic but told the priest that there was no doubt that Father Kapaun should be made a Saint. He based his opinion on two key findings—the first was that fewer men died at Camp No. 5 than other prison camps. The second was the fact that the stories about the heroics and compassion of Father Kapaun had not changed over time. Over the years, O'Brien had developed an ability to separate the truth from the, well, embellishments. He could recognize the accounts that got better over beers at the VFW hall as they were passed from veteran to veteran. Not so with Father Kapaun. Over hundreds of hours of interviews and reviewing written accounts, O'Brien found that the stories about the chaplain were told as consistently as they first were by his fellow prisoners back in 1953.

No conflation. No inflation.

"So, Phil asks me, 'Do you mind if I talk to you a little bit about some stuff I've been thinking about?'" said Father Hotze.

The priest had been as interested in hearing from O'Brien then as I was now.

O'Brien had then told Father Hotze, "I am more and more convinced that on the day that Father Kapaun was captured in Korea that he came to the conclusion that he knew that he was going to die.

"And right then he decided his mission in life was to help as many people as he could. So, from that point on, it did not matter when he died. It did not matter how he died. He knew that he was going to die and was able to help people without having any fear.

"It gave him the courage to push the gun pointed at Miller's head away and the strength to carry him on his back for days," O'Brien had said. "It didn't matter if he got caught stealing food or breaking into the enlisted men's quarters. He knew he was going to die. It was in God's hands. What mattered was helping as many people as he could until then."

As O'Brien went on, Father Hotze had found himself thinking about the Gospel of St. John, especially the Passion and how Jesus took control of the situation.

Hotze now said to me, "When he is asked if he is King of the Jews, he answers, 'Who do you think I am?' Eventually, he tells them that he is God. Then we see Jesus's suffering and how he gave up his spirit. It isn't that they are killing him, but Jesus is choosing to give up his life for us."

Like Jesus, Father Kapaun was willing to give up his life for his fellow men. On that, Father Hotze agreed with O'Brien. But Hotze had told his friend that he perhaps was wrong about when Father Kapaun decided to die for others.

"How can you say that it was on the day that he was captured?" Father Hotze had asked him. "I think Father Kapaun made that decision well before that. What's to say that he did not make that decision when he landed in Korea? We have heard the good things he did long before he was captured. How he dodged bullets and dove in fox-holes to care for the wounded. How he gave comfort and respect to Jews and Protestants. How he shared his time, his kindness. When he re-enlisted in the military—how do you know that that wasn't the day he decided he was going to give himself for others?

"How can you say he didn't make that decision when he became a priest? When he decided he was going to give his all for the people of Pilsen and become the best parish priest possible? How can you know that he didn't make that decision even before that? When he was growing up and going to school and helping his classmates with their studies or helping his mom and dad on the farm so they could have money and make it through the Depression? I think he made this decision well before that.

"What I have taken away from all this work on Father Kapaun is this," Father Hotze continued. "While people hear what a hero he was in the military, I believe his valor came from the virtue that had been instilled in him early in his life. He spent his whole life giving himself up for other people. He lived his whole life following the example of Christ and laying down his life for others. And that's why he is a saint."

11

No sincere prayer is ever wasted," Father Kapaun once said.

It was a sentiment, a promise, that had stuck with me throughout the time I spent reporting, understanding, and contemplating the priest's life. A reassuring promise, yes? It should be, and for a great many I am sure it is. For me, however, those six words sat stuck in my throat not unlike a swallow of scotch whiskey that went down the wrong pipe. It should be tasty, comforting, a small miracle, but instead it burns and makes me cough and frown.

Now, in neither case is there something flawed or false in God's promise or that barrel of whiskey. Rather, it is my problem. Somewhere along the way I lost my way—not my faith or belief in God—but how to convey it to Him or to center my life around Him.

This fact hit me between the eyes when I had my

initial lunch with Father Martin, the Jesuit priest, writer, and editor, and was unable to articulate how, or if, I prayed. He had sensed my discomfort.

"Prayer should be an exercise in being honest with God and asking for his help," he'd said.

I had not been doing that. I didn't know how. Like a golfer who suddenly cannot make a twelve-inch putt or a second baseman who cannot make a short throw to first base, I had developed the "yips" when it came to talking to my God. I was tongue-tied and twisted.

Like the errant duffer who still loved golf and the spooked second baseman who still loved baseball, I was still passionate about faith. I was not going to develop better skills, greater comfort, or a deeper love and understanding about my relationship with God without severe course corrections. But how? Which was more daunting—realizing you are bereft of a vital spiritual connection or figuring out a way to restore it?

One of my greatest takeaways from journalism is that momentum prompts questions, which in turn leads you to answers. When you are chasing a lead or reporting out a story, you pick up the phone and call people who know more about it than you do. You read everything you can about a topic. The saying "a mile wide and an inch deep" is meant for journalists. You get comfortable knowing what you don't know while at the same time becoming more confident that the right questions are bubbling up inside you. That, in turn, means you have a better chance of finding the person with the right answers. You keep moving. You keep casting a wide net. You report out the story and follow where it leads.

In Father Kapaun, I had a near-perfect example of prayer and sacrifice. In Father Hotze, I had a theologian and scholar who could distill the would-be saint's virtue.

The problem was that I was operating at a sixth-grade spiritual level while being thrown into the deep end of the beatific pool. I needed a better foundation to understand them. I needed to understand myself before I could understand them. So I went back to the basics—I revisited the Bible and the Baltimore Catechism, reread *The Power of Your Subconscious Mind* along with other books that had made an impact on me at various times in my life: *The Artist's Way* by Julia Cameron and *Grace (Eventually)* by Anne Lamott. I dipped in and out of Thomas Merton's *The Seven Storey Mountain*. I read, listened to, and tried on the Christian mysticism of Father Richard Rohr, a Franciscan priest whose ability to convey the joys of contemplation, compassion, and activism for the marginalized have made him wildly popular.

I was riveted by the memoir *Priestdaddy* by Patricia Lockwood about growing up and eventually returning home as an adult to live with her father—a guitar playing former navy sailor who likes to lounge in his boxers and is a married Catholic priest. Father Lockwood was a Lutheran minister married to a Catholic, and he was granted a papal dispensation after he accepted his call to the priesthood. It is a human, funny look at the ties, troubles, and triumphs of family and how they are impossibly held together by love. Beyond being a man in full, with the good and bad that entails, Father Lockwood offers memorable teachings. This is the one that sticks with me the most: "Good theology teaches you that everyone belongs to themselves." Then he turned to his daughter and said, "You come from us, but you're not us."

Long after I read the book, I discovered Father Lockwood is the pastor at my childhood parish in Kansas City, Christ the King, the same place I met my first priest, Monsignor Kearney. He also taught at Kenrick Seminary in St. Louis where Father Kapaun and Monsignor Kearney studied for the priesthood.

My spiritual antennae were up, and I found inspiration—or at least something to think about—in unusual places. On an irreverent sports podcast, *Pardon My Take*, the actor Gary Busey offered a soliloquy on faith and Christ. He spoke with the ardor of a preacher, one whose life was the stuff of tabloid fodder: a best-actor Academy Award nomination, a near-fatal motorcycle accident, drug overdoses and rehab visits, and, finally, a triumph over cancer. Busey said that he believed in heaven. Hell, now that was trickier. "Hell exists for people who need religion," he said. "Spirituality is for people who have already been there."

On another podcast, I discovered the work and world

of Rachel Held Evans. She was a contemporary, accessible, and edgy voice for the Christians, or "doubt-filled believers." She grew up in the evangelical community but became uncomfortable about how intolerant it was of women and the LGBTQ community. She was progressive and transparent about her struggles finding comfort in her beliefs. Evans wanted everyone to be better, more inclusive, and kinder. Being a believer was hard enough; why should church leaders and hierarchies make it harder?

In 2019, she died from an unexpected illness at the age of thirty-seven, leaving a husband, two small children, and a following that, through her, had found a seat at the Lord's table. At her funeral in Chattanooga, Tennessee, Reverend Nadia Bolz-Weber, a Lutheran pastor, quoted Evans's own words in her benediction.

"Jesus invites us into a story bigger than ourselves and our imaginations," she said. "May we never lose our love for telling the story."

I also sought out the people I have known and admired for their steadfast faith. We have all come across them. They are from all walks of life. When I was a kid, I thought they were scary, strange even, for going to Mass or working their rosary beads daily. Growing up, I had friends who got ribbed and were frequently embarrassed by their parents' piety. It stood out perhaps more in the Midwest where reserve is a desired trait and a person's faith was between him and his God. While attending college in Texas and working throughout the South, I became used to hearing professions of faith: the God blesses; I'm saved; I'll pray for you. It was part of the cultural fabric and a signifier with a long and honored tradition. I became more comfortable with these displays and recognized they were for the most part sincere.

What all of these deeply faithful individuals shared was a serenity and sense of joy and confidence. Growing older, I recognized more frequently these traits and envied all who possessed them. They did not fluff their angel wings or polish their halos or stand atop the church steps preaching about the right way. Instead, they endured the deaths of spouses or children and battled their own terrible diseases. Still, they bounced back, their joyfulness intact. Many I watched die, including my own parents, and they did so with grace and peace and acceptance that they had lived good lives and were off to a better place. All of this is about faith.

I have a friend named Bob Berner who is pushing ninety and continues to live life like he does not have a care in the world. My wife, who grew up with his daughter, tells me that he has been that way ever since she could remember. He graduated from the University of Notre Dame, got a law degree at Harvard University, married his wife, Sheila, and had five children who in turn gave him twenty-one grandchildren. Bob fills up a room with his shock of white hair and lighthouse smile.

He loves being around people. He peppers them with questions. He tells stories.

Bob still travels from his home in Chicago to New York, Florida, or Wyoming for every family baptism, wedding, and graduation. Sheila was always with him even as Alzheimer's stole away her mind. For the past couple years, however, Sheila has needed round-the-clock care and doesn't travel. Bob is home with her most of the day. He goes to Mass every day—always has. He is devout. Bob won't tell you that, but you can recognize it by the way he attacks life each day. Bob has thought a lot about the Catholic Church and his own faith. He has done pro bono legal work for the Diocese of Chicago. He has been a board member or volunteer at many of Chicago's Catholic seminaries and institutions. He is a supporter and reader of *Commonweal*, the oldest independent Roman Catholic journal of opinion. It is liberal, as is Bob. He knows his church history. He reads its current thinkers and writers. He is heartbroken by the sexual abuse scandal and the lives it has ruined. As nuanced as is his understanding of the Church, Bob is black-and-white when it comes to his faith.

"It's not a political party—you don't pick and choose a side," he said. "My faith is who I am. It is not dented because of the horrible things done by clergy. I'm the church, too. We all are the church, not just the guys wearing robes and beanies."

As a young man, Bob had his doubts. He remembers tossing and turning late one night, agitated and depressed, wondering if there really was a God. Bob thought about it. He prayed on it. Then a powerful peace settled over him. Yes, there was a God.

"I could feel it," he said. "Now when I go to Mass, I might spend the first twenty minutes fretting about one thing or another—Sheila, the kids, the fact I'm old. But usually, before Communion, I find this peace. It's maybe for thirty seconds. But it's worth it."

I took a step in the right direction after my oldest brother, Tom, gave me *Give Us This Day*, a small, sleek missalette. It is a cross between an old-fashioned prayer book and new-age inspiration. It comes out monthly, and it offers some scripture, prayers, and even the Mass liturgy for each day of the week. It leans on the Gospels of Jesus Christ but also is sprinkled with monastic wisdom and spiritual reflections. In short, its pages are a buffet for various spiritual tastes. Like everything else in the world, you can download the app, which I eventually did after the books started piling up. It is published by Liturgical Press, which was founded in 1926 by the Benedictine monks of Saint John's Abbey in Collegeville, Minnesota.

This little book gave me some footing for prayer. It took me a while, but I finally settled into a routine of spending ten to fifteen minutes opening my pathways for prayer in the hope of capturing Bob's thirty seconds of comfort or reassurance.

I start with the "Blessed Among Us" section of the day because, well, I believe that is why my brother gave the missalette to me, and it was a handy piece of research besides. These are mini profiles of saints or people worth emulating because they lived their lives in the service of others. Not all of them are Catholic—Martin Luther King Jr. and Mohandas Gandhi and other contemporary figures get their due as well. Not all of them are relatable, especially the saints from the Middle Ages who took to caves or basement cells to live on bread and water and prayer.

In these small portraits written by Robert Ellsberg, however, is a rich history of the Catholic Church, warts and all. And after more than a year of reading them, one of the most confounding things for me was how tone-deaf the Church has been for centuries. How the hierarchy, from popes to pastors, has failed to practice what Jesus preached and lived, especially when it came to women. Jesus revered his mother Mary, offered Mary Magdalene his friendship and respect, and treated women as equals and kindly throughout scripture. So why have women been treated as second-class citizens throughout time? Their contributions to the Church and society is enormous and often was accomplished against great opposition of the male hierarchy. There are multiple instances of this lack of regard throughout time. Let's take one: Sister Mary MacKillop, the founder of the Sisters of St. Joseph of the Sacred Heart.

Here is her "Blessed Among Us" entry.

With her beatification in 1995, Mary MacKillop became the first recognized saint of Australia. She was the founder of a remarkable congregation, the Sisters of St. Joseph, who devoted themselves to providing free education and other services to the poor in the rugged conditions of rural Australia. Her congregation would adhere to a strict vow of poverty; there would be no social distinctions within the order; and the congregation would be subject to an elected mother general, rather than the local bishop. This latter provision became a source of grave tension between the congregation and the Australian bishops.

Mary's congregation was approved by Rome and quickly attracted scores of young women. At a time when almost no public services were available for the poor, the work of the sisters was widely admired. But the harassment from local bishops quickly reached extraordinary lengths. Mary was subjected to a shameless campaign of vilification and at one point was excommunicated. Nevertheless, Rome supported her constitutions and she was completely vindicated. Throughout her sufferings she remained free of bitterness. Innocent suffering, she believed, was an opportunity to shoulder the cross and grow closer to God. Those who caused this suffering were thus her "most powerful benefactors." When she died on

August 8, 1909, her passing was mourned throughout Australia. Mary was canonized in 2010.

Beyond the history lessons, the "Blessed Among Us" snapshots offer inspiration from their subjects and in their own words: "Care and perplexities form part of my life but I am learning to look upon them as I think God wishes and so I am happy," from Sister Mary MacKillop (1842–1909).

After reading about the lives of saints, or would-be saints, I opt for the meat and potatoes of worship that was part of my upbringing: a psalm and an Old Testament scripture. If nothing else, the nuns were big on structure. It is the petitions, or prayers offered for others, written by Sister Susan Barber, OSB, that never fail to move me. Praying for others, praying for a better world. Even though these petitions are mass-produced weeks or months ahead of time, it's uncanny how they feel in the moment.

"Give your Church courage and confidence to welcome all people with unconditional love and hospitality."

"Good and forgiving God, hear our prayer."

Sometimes, I think they were meant for me.

"Inspire reporters, journalists, and social media users to communicate with respect and a love for truth."

"O God, make haste to help us."

"Help us truly listen to one another, without fear, and lead us to embrace your truth together."

"God, in your mercy, hear our prayer."

"Prosper and advance fruitful and intelligent dialogue among our nation's leaders."

"Let us find our joy in you, O God."

Finally, I end with the brief spiritual reflections the app offers each day. Each reflection is three hundred words or so. Like the entries in the "Blessed Among Us" selections, these writings reflect a range of thinking from the Middle Ages to modern times, and they come from everyone from Pope Francis to Julian of Norwich, a fifteenth-century English mystic. There are contemporary priests and nuns who adapt writings and exercises they have incorporated into their work as spiritual retreat leaders, like Michael Casey, a Cistercian monk of Tarrawarra Abbey in Australia. There are passages from the archives of more well-known spiritual figures, such as Dorothy Day, a social justice advocate and cofounder of the Catholic Worker movement.

There are spiritual nudges.

"What can we do?" writes Day. "We can pray. We can pray without ceasing, as St. Paul said. We can say with the Apostles, 'Lord, teach me to pray.' We can say with St. Paul, 'Lord, what wilt Thou have me to do?'"

There's wisdom.

"As I have grown old, my feelings about God have tapered down to gratitude and hope. Gratitude is the pleasure of hope come true," writes the late author and ethics and theology professor Lewis B. Smedes in his spiritual memoir *My God and I*, excerpted in *Give Us This Day*.

"Hope is the pain of gratitude postponed. Gratitude comes easy, on its own steam, whenever we know that someone has given us a real gift. Hope comes harder, sometimes with our backs against the wall, laden with doubts that what we hope for will ever come. Gratitude always feels good, as close to joy as any feeling can get. Hope can feel unbearable; when we passionately long for what we do not have and it is taking too long to come, we are restless as a farmer waiting for rain after an August without a drop."

There are some beautiful thoughts and writings available in *Give Us This Day*. After reading "The Long Good-Bye," a small essay by Kathleen Norris about the Ascension of Mary, I wanted to know more about this poet-essayist, especially after reading the poem she wrote that was the basis for the essay. The poem is called "Ascension" and it still takes my breath away, especially its last line.

Why do you stand looking up at the skies?
Acts 1:11

It wasn't just wind, chasing
the gunmetal clouds
across the loud sky;

it wasn't the feeling that one might ascend
on that excited air,
rising like a trumpet note.

And it wasn't just my sister's water breaking,
her crying out,
the downward draw of blood and bone . . .

It was all of that,
the mud and new grass
pushing up through melting snow,
the lilac in bud
by my front door, bent low
by last week's ice storm.

Now the new mother, that leaky vessel,
begins to nurse her child,
beginning the long good-bye.

So, with the help of this little prayer book, I was making my way toward sincere prayer, step by step, day by day. It was progress.

12

The General Curia of the Society of Jesus—the Jesuit headquarters—is just a few hundred feet from St. Peter's Square, but it is not in Vatican City proper. Nor is it part of the Holy See, the worldwide government of the Catholic Church, which is recognized as a sovereign juridical entity. Nonetheless, it is very much part of the Catholic Church. It gets the same protection and services as the offices and residences within the walls of the Vatican. The Jesuits' General Curia lacks the architecture and opulence of its neighbors. The brick building was constructed in 1927, and its interiors have the feel of an oversized parochial grade school—austere and utilitarian. Wood desks and benches. Metal file cabinets. Footsteps echo in its wide hallways. The smell of disinfectant creeps in your nose.

It is a vibe and aesthetic that I expected from a religious order that was founded by a wealthy nobleman-turned-soldier with a big enough ego to seek and win military glory before doing a 180-degree turn to embrace self-denial and study, spirituality, and rigorous thinking. It is stripped down of any adornments. Its founder, Saint Ignatius Loyola, after all, had stripped down his fortunes and ambitions, and altered his thinking to create the Society of Jesus. This spiritual awakening unfolded over two decades of wandering and prayer that culminated shortly after he was ordained a priest with a vision. One day, deep in prayer, Ignatius saw Christ with the cross on his shoulder, and beside him was the Father.

"I wish you to take this man for your servant," God told Jesus.

"My will is that you should serve us," Jesus said to Ignatius.

Why did a wealthy and worldly Spaniard from a noble family turn his back on all the comforts and success he had had? To find God—and help others do the same.

It started at age thirty, when he took a cannonball to a leg on May 20, 1521, at the Battle of Pamplona. That led to a botched operation, a long convalescence, and hours reading about the life of Christ as well as the lives of several saints. The following year, Ignatius began to wander—to a monastery in Montserrat in northeastern Spain where he confessed his sins and laid down his sword and dagger near the statue of the Virgin Mary. He went to Manresa near Barcelona, and, for nearly a year, he barely ate or drank. He took to the streets to beg. He attended daily Mass. He prayed.

Jerusalem was next. Ignatius set out in late March 1523 and, after stops in Rome, Venice, and Cyprus, reached the Holy City on September 4, 1523. He saw Christ's touchstones—Bethlehem, Bethany, the Jordan River, the Mount of Olives, and Mount of Temptation. He worked on his faith, his spirituality, writing notes for a book that would become the *Spiritual Exercises*. Things he believed. A how-to book about opening your heart and mind to become closer to Jesus Christ. He had meditations, contemplations, prayers, and exercises to not only acknowledge that Christ was with you in all things, but to recognize him, feel him, talk to him. The hallmark of this book was his encouraging people to imagine themselves in scenes from the Gospels, to "compose the place" in their mind's eye, and in that imagining, encounter Christ.

He left a month later and reached Barcelona in March 1524, where he spent the first two of twelve years in classrooms. Along the way, he picked up followers. There were others like him who wanted more. He caught the attention of the authorities. He was arrested, braced about what he was teaching, and arrested for heresy a couple times—once even doing a stint in prison.

Ignatius left Spain and arrived in Paris on February 2, 1528. He remained until 1535. He studied more, earning a degree in religious studies at the Collège de

Sainte-Barbe in the Latin Quarter. He meditated, contemplated, and prayed. He kept afloat by begging for alms from Spanish merchants or anyone else. He found more friends or followers or, in any case, like-minded spiritualists—among them another Spaniard from a noble family, Francisco de Jasso y Azpilicueta, who would help found the Society of Jesus with Ignatius and, still later, become Saint Francis Xavier, one of the Church's greatest missionaries.

On August 15, 1534, in a crypt beneath the Church of Saint Denis in the Montmartre area of Paris, Ignatius and his six like-minded friends decided to pronounce the vows of poverty, chastity, and obedience. Ignatius was not yet ordained as a priest, and though the founding of the Society of Jesus may have seemed inevitable, it was several years off. To others, it may have seemed improbable, given some of the opposition that Ignatius was already facing for his innovative ideas on prayer.

Ignatius next went to Spain and then Italy and studied in Venice. In early January of 1537, his Paris friends met him in Venice with the intention of going to Jerusalem to convert the infidels. But war with the Ottoman Empire grounded them in Italy. On June 24, 1537, Ignatius and his subsequent cofounders were ordained as priests in Venice, where they remained for eighteen months while figuring out how best to be servants of Christ, or, as they called one another, Friends in the Lord.

By 1540, Ignatius and his friends, working from Rome,

asked Pope Paul III to approve their plan to become a religious order obedient to the pope. Ignatius was the obvious choice to lead them. The Society of Jesus was to be a "ready to live in any part of the world where there was hope of God's greater glory and the good of souls" order, and the training of new members, Jesuits, would be as long and rigorous as Ignatius's was. Today, Jesuit training from start to finish can take as much as twenty years.

The Jesuits mushroomed quickly under Ignatius's leadership; by the time he died in 1556, there were nearly one thousand of them spread across Italy, Spain, Germany, France, and Portugal, as well as India and Brazil, the Congo and Ethiopia. From the outset, the fearlessness and discipline of Jesuits earned them their nicknames: God's Soldiers, the Pope's Marines, the Long Black Line, or the Company. In 1609, fifty-four years after his death, Ignatius was beatified by Pope Paul V, and in 1622 he was canonized by Pope Gregory XV. In 1922, he was declared patron of all spiritual retreats by Pope Pius XI.

Today, the Jesuits are among the largest religious orders of priests and brothers in the Catholic Church, with nearly sixteen thousand members in 112 countries on six continents. The most famous among them lived on the other side of the Vatican wall: Jorge Mario Bergoglio, the former Jesuit novice director better known as Pope Francis.

Now another Jesuit was standing before me, Father Pascual Cebollada Silvestre, the postulator, or man who argued and advocated for the sainthood for selected members of the Society of Jesus. I met him in early February 2019, and he had been appointed about two years prior in March 2017. He confessed early in our conversation that he was new to the job and still trying to figure out the pathways to eternal divinity. He, too, was from Spain and, by his own admission, was that rare Jesuit who accepted his calling early, entering the Jesuit order one year after finishing high school in Madrid in 1978 and pursuing the life of the soul and mind determinedly. Cebollada was ordained in 1989. He earned degrees in philosophy and theology from the Comillas Pontifical University in Madrid, and he defended his doctoral thesis in theology at the Centre Sèvres in Paris in 1993. Cebollada returned to the Comillas Pontifical University and taught courses in theory and practice of the spiritual exercises, spiritual discernment, spiritual direction, and spiritual theology. He was a theologian, a philosopher, and—perhaps not surprisingly, being the son of a film critic and author—an accomplished writer.

I had come to see Father Cebollada for an overview of the Congregation for the Causes of Saints and his impressions of the Saint-making machinery. He knew that I was Jesuit-educated and was writing about Father Kapaun. He had checked with his American colleagues and was delighted to tell me that the Jesuits had founded the all-boys school in Wichita named for Father Kapaun. In fact, the school was founded in 1956 with money raised by Father Kapaun's fellow prisoners of war who wanted to honor the priest and remembered that he had vowed to donate his army back pay to the children of the Diocese of Wichita.

Cebollada had black hair marbled by a few white strands and wore rimless glasses. He was soft-spoken but had an easy way about him and was quick to smile, especially when it came to the adventure that was his new job. He joked that he was a regular visitor to the offices of the Congregation for the Causes of Saints, partly because he had so many questions, partly because he had to redo so many tasks.

"The greatest quality required is patience—things move slowly, and the rules and formats are exact," Cebollada said. "But they have been patient with me as well as I learn on the job. So far it has been an interesting and good experience. But I am not an expert postulator."

Cebollada had an important job, and the shoes he was filling were big ones, as would be the shoes he would someday leave behind for his eventual successor. Over the centuries, the Jesuits have proved to be very effective postulators for members of their order. There are 53 Jesuits who have been canonized as Saints, with another 154 designated as Blessed. There were about one hundred causes of Jesuits whose files are open in the Congregation for the Causes of Saints. Some were "asleep," meaning they had failed to catch the imagination of local populations enough to spur devotion and momentum. Others were active. Cebollada was awaiting a miracle to be proven for a Jesuit in Mexico, another in Germany, and another in Spain to push them over the Saint finish line.

Still, on February 12, 2019, Father Cebollada was having a good day. He had just gotten word that the Holy Father had authorized the Congregation for the Causes of Saints to authorize the beatification of an Ecuadorian martyr, Father Emilio Moscoso, as well as to confirm the heroic virtues of Father Manuel García Nieto, a Spanish Jesuit. While Father Nieto, a spiritual director and teacher devoted to his seminarians in Spain, had been deemed to have lived his life heroically, it was Father Moscoso who was knocking on heaven's door.

Father Moscoso was born on August 21, 1846, in Ecuador and assassinated during the country's Liberal Revolution when the government was openly hostile to the Catholic Church and targeted priests. He had studied as a lawyer, was ordained at the age of thirty-one, and became a noted theologian, philosopher, and university professor. In the predawn hours of May 4, 1897, soldiers broke down the door of the Jesuit house located near the college in the town of Riobamba where Moscoso taught. They killed everyone in their way and broke into the tabernacle to drink the wine and toss the Communion hosts—the small wafers that Catholics believe become the body of Christ—as a sign of disrespect for the sacraments. Father Moscoso was in his room, kneeling before a crucifix and praying the rosary. The soldiers shot him twice in the head. The colonel in charge dragged his body into the street but was confronted by angry people, including some of his soldiers, outraged by his brutality.

The cause of Father Moscoso was opened in 1997 and moved quickly as cases of martyrs, or people who give their lives defending their faith, often do. It helped that Father Moscoso was a Jesuit, but more important was the fact that he was from South America, a part of the world where contemporary Catholic priests were in short supply and as a result the Church was losing Catholics to the growing evangelical movement. The evangelicals had more boots on the ground, and Saint-making has become a powerful weapon in the tug-of-war to wrest more souls into the Catholic Church. Pope Francis, who was born and rose through the Jesuit and then archdiocesan ranks in Argentina, was aware of the need to shore up his home continent. There are other continents that need help getting their spiritual heroes recognized as well.

"There are priorities like South America, Asia, and Africa," acknowledged Father Cebollada, "and the process continues to evolve."

In 2014, at Pope Francis's direction, the Congregation for the Causes of Saints put financial limits in place to ensure fairness. Among salacious allegations of corruption, jealousy, and misconduct under Pope Benedict XVI that were leaked to Italian newspapers in 2012 was the suggestion that financially well-backed causes moved—if not to the front of the line—a lot more quickly than the saintly candidates from poorer regions of the world.

According to the Vatican's official newspaper, *L'Osservatore Romano*, the cost-reduction effort was a response to the pope's request to standardize the canonization process and provide more public information on the costs associated with it. Pope Francis wants to (a) provide assistance to dioceses and religious orders that are unable to raise the funding for their causes, and (b) create a preferential pathway for Saint candidates who are not well known, as well as benefit victims of the Nazi and Communist persecutions of the twentieth century.

Among the first to benefit from these standards was Bishop Óscar Arnulfo Romero of El Salvador. From 1977 until his death in 1980, Romero was the Archbishop of San Salvador and an outspoken critic of the country's violent right-wing regime that had left El Salvador deeply poor and riven by social injustice. Torture and assassinations were common. On March 24, 1980, Romero delivered a sermon appealing to Salvadoran soldiers to obey God, not the government, and stop repressing the freedoms and human rights of their fellow citizens.

"No soldier is bound to follow orders that contradict the law of God. Don't you see; you are killing your own brothers and sisters," he said. "I beg you; I implore you; I order you: stop the repression!"

Later that evening, while celebrating Mass in the small chapel of a hospital for cancer patients and the terminally ill, Bishop Romero was gunned down. No one was ever convicted for the crime, but the Commission on the Truth for El Salvador subsequently concluded that the assassination was ordered by a right-wing politician and death-squad leader by the name of Roberto D'Aubuisson.

The cause of Archbishop Romero was much debated and had stalled under Popes John Paul II and Benedict XVI, both of whom were uncomfortable with what they considered Romero's far-left views and perceived embrace of "liberation theology," which sees Christ as a liberator of those who are oppressed—a thoroughly Christian idea that was often wrongly equated with Marxism.

But Archbishop Romero's work and compassion for the marginalized had inspired Pope Francis as a young priest. Two years after Francis became pope, he beat-ified Archbishop Romero. He was canonized by Pope Francis—three years later—on October 24, 2018. At Romero's canonization ceremony in St. Peter's Square, Francis wore the blood-stained rope belt that Romero had worn on the evening of his assassination, and said the bishop had "left the security of the world, even his own safety, in order to give his life according to the gospel—close to the poor and to his people."

Earlier, in February 2018, Father Cebollada called on Cardinal Giovanni Angelo Becciu, the prefect of the Congregation for the Causes of Saints. An important part of the job of a postulator is lobbying on behalf of one's candidates. Father Cebollada had been urged by his superiors to press for the cause of Father Moscoso as well as that of Father Eusebio Francisco Kino, an Italian Jesuit, missionary and explorer, mapmaker and astronomer, who died in 1711 at age sixty-five. During the last twenty-four years of his life, Padre Kino, as he was known, mapped and charted what is now southern Arizona and Sonora, Mexico, working with more than a dozen Native American tribes. He disproved the belief at the time that the Baja California Peninsula was an island and led an overland expedition there. Padre Kino parted with fellow missionaries on the Spaniards' policy of slavery, opposing the forced labor of the tribes in their silver mines. He also established twenty-four missions and chapels in the territory before he died.

"It's a lovely case," said Father Cebollada. "He straddled cultures and brought people together all while doing important work as an explorer. They called him the Marco Polo of the Americas."

Padre Kino had not been designated a Servant of God yet, the first step in the process of sainthood, and Father Cebollada was hoping to get his cause in front of Cardinal Becciu and persuade him that the causes of both Moscoso and Kino needed to move more quickly.

As prefect, Cardinal Becciu was not only the head of the congregation, but the man who decided the order and pace of the causes in the pipeline to be heard. Ultimately, though, Cardinal Becciu was the key to getting any individual cause in front of the Holy Father. Cardinal Becciu, of course, leaned on his staff. He had a secretary, an undersecretary, and a staff of twenty-three people at his disposal. The congregation itself is made up of thirty-four members—cardinals, archbishops, and bishops—a Promoter of the Faith (or prelate theologian), five relators, and eighty-three consultors. That's not much manpower considering that there are more than two thousand causes in the pipeline.

"With Father Moscoso, I apparently made a good case. But with Father Kino, I wasn't so lucky," Cebollada said with a shrug. "The cardinal said two or three more years."

Father Cebollada developed an appreciation for the Saint-making process immediately after taking a five-month class required of new postulators by the Congregation for the Causes of Saints. He understood why certain templates and the hierarchy must be followed. He laughed while he told me that Pope Benedict had mandated a reduction in the number of pages of an individual *positio*: to under five hundred, even shorter if possible.

"It is in his nature as a scholar that he read every word of the *positio* of the causes that he was considering," said Father Cebollada.

A cause's first hurdle is to get past the historians, a pool of sixty or so. The pool consists of a mix of clerics and laypeople drawn from all corners of the world. They are broken down into panels of six, assigned by expertise. For Father Kino, for example, it would be experts in the Americas as wells as in the histories of exploration and cartography.

"They are a resource as well as judges—they can point us to archives that might have been overlooked where important papers may be held," said Father Cebollada. "For them, it is an intellectual exercise. Do we have a complete picture of this man or woman's place in history or society? Do we have all their writings? Do we know all their achievements?"

Next, theologians examine the cause. They, too, are drawn from a wide pool of scholars of religious studies, philosophy, spirituality, and religious texts. They are assigned into a nine-member panel appropriate to the individual cause. If the candidate left homilies or writings, the panel parses them for solid theology and sanctity. The theologians, too, want to ensure the postulators put their best foot forward on behalf of their cause. In fact, on the cause of Father Nieto, the panel suggested that Father Cebollada reframe part of his *positio*. Father Nieto was a spiritual father and professor of pastoral and spiritual theology at the Comillas Pontifical University, where he was beloved by his students and earned the name Father of the Poor for his work among the disadvantaged in the community until he died in 1974.

"He was an old-school Jesuit and spiritual instructor who had a formal and courtly way about him, and in some of his writings," said Father Cebollada. "Because of that, they were concerned that Father Nieto had not accepted and embraced Vatican II, or hadn't changed with the times. When I explained this wasn't the case at all, they suggested I try again and try to present his image in a more modern way."

The panel also examines witness statements for authenticity and powerful testimony. The bar is high, especially when examined through the lens of the seven virtues. Was he or she chaste, pure, or abstinent if they took a vow that required it? Did they observe temperance, display humanity and a giving spirit? Were they charitable and benevolent, and did they sacrifice for others? Did they display diligence or a persistent effort to live every day ethically? Did their life demonstrate patience, and did they forgive and extend mercy? Was kindness and compassion part of their everyday life? Were they guided by humility, and were they reverent and brave?

Sure, Father Cebollada conceded that he would prefer a more streamlined process that moved more quickly, but time and rigor was required because the bar to sainthood is rightly set high.

"Like the sacraments, this is the mediation between

our faith and our God," he said. "The saints are part of the incarnation of God. When we make Saints, we are saying that each reproduces the life of Christ."

Father Cebollada was in the beginning stages of a cause that was very important to him as well as all in the Jesuit order: that of Father Pedro Arrupe, the twenty-eighth Superior General of the Society of Jesus and widely considered the architect of the modernization of the order. He coined the term "men for others" that remains a rallying cry for Jesuit-run schools like the one that I attended, and that my son now attends. (As the Jesuits began opening coed schools, that motto evolved into "men and women for others.") Father Arrupe was the society's leader as it navigated Vatican II—the Church's effort to be more contemporary and accessible—and he renewed the order's commitment to the poor as well as weighting their mission in favor of social justice. Along the way he founded the Jesuit Refugee Service, which today helps millions of refugees, migrants, and displaced persons worldwide.

"Our faith in Jesus Christ and our mission to proclaim the Gospel demand of us a commitment to promote justice and enter into solidarity with the voiceless and the powerless," he wrote in "Our Mission Today: The Service of Faith and the Promotion of Justice."

In the 1970s and '80s, this endorsement of social justice by Father Arrupe put the Jesuits at odds with more conservative church officials and put some of his colleagues in physical danger, especially in Latin American countries run by strongmen and military juntas. In 1977, Father Rutilio Grande, a practitioner of liberation theology, was assassinated in El Salvador. In 1989, six Jesuits, along with their housekeeper and her daughter, were murdered at the Jesuit University of Central America in El Salvador.

Father Cebollada told me that Father Arrupe was also a profound influence on Pope Francis—that the two knew each other and it was Father Arrupe who had appointed the then young Jesuit as the provincial superior of the Society of Jesus in Argentina on July 31, 1973.

"So, this cause will be fast-tracked?" I asked, citing the speed in which Mother Teresa was canonized as well as the glide path afforded Father Moscoso.

Father Cebollada shook his head vigorously.

"No, of course not," he said. "The pope is the ultimate judge and he can only decide at the end of the process, no matter how well he knew him."

Nine months after our meeting, on November 7, 2019, at a gathering of Jesuits at the Vatican's apostolic palace, Pope Francis spoke movingly of Father Arrupe and reaffirmed the Society of Jesuits' commitment to social justice. He quoted a line from one of the late superior general's writings: "I saw God so close to those who suffer, to those who cry, to those who are shipwrecked on this life of abandonment, that it sparked in me the burning desire to imitate him in this voluntary closeness to the discarded of the world, which society despises."

Pope Francis said Father Arrupe was a "man of prayer, a man who wrestled with God every day, and from hence comes this strength."

Father Arrupe always believed that the service of faith and the promotion of justice cannot be separated: "They are radically united," the pope told them.

Now, back in the Curia, before we headed to a trattoria for a pizza, Father Cebollada wanted me to see something. It was not the roof of the building, which is said to have a stunning view of the glittering dome of St. Peter's Basilica, or the Curia's hidden terraced garden. We did, however, stop into the chapel that was the heart of the Jesuit headquarters, where the relics—the bones or personal belongings of the holy men and women, in this case sixteen Jesuit saints—rested. Then Father Cebollada took me inside what looked like a supply room with dented file cabinets and a wardrobe. The postulator showed me the shoes and suit once worn by Father Arrupe—one day in the future, hopefully, they would be relics of a saint. He handed me a small case containing a bone of Saint Ignatius, but that was not what he was looking for, either.

Instead, Father Cebollada pulled out a human skull. It belonged to Andrew of Phu Yen, a Vietnamese boy who assisted French Jesuit missionaries before being killed at the age of twenty in 1644 for refusing to refute his faith. Before he was beheaded at a public execution in Kẻ Chàm, Vietnam, Andrew's last word was to cry out Jesus's name. He was Vietnam's first martyr, and he was beatified by Pope John Paul II on March 5, 2000.

Father Cebollada told me that at least a couple times a month a group of Vietnamese showed up at the Curia unannounced. They were from Canada, or the Philippines, France, or the United States. They wanted to see Andrew's skull. So Father Cebollada would get it out of here and say a Mass with them. Sometimes, they merely wanted to touch the skull, bow their head, and pray. The point, he said, is no matter how poor or humble, people wanted to see themselves in God.

"When you confront poverty or austerity with sanctity, that is powerful. Andrew was one of them. They love him. We all need models of sanctity," he said. "They are the best images of Christ. They are the best of all of us. That is why we need saints."

13

Dr. Andrea Ambrosi is a big man, standing six-foot-two with broad shoulders, and he looked even bigger as he stood in his small office near the Piazza Navona. His black suit and maroon tie knotted tight was at odds with this neighborhood of sidewalk trattorias, bakeries, and small tourist shops. In fact, I had walked past his address, Via Tor Millina 19, a couple of times without noticing the three-story building. His office was on the second floor at the top of a staircase. It reminded me of my late father's law office—a small, dark reception area, heavy wood desk, stiff-backed chairs, overflowing bookshelves, and an ever-so-faint smell of must. The Miracle Hunter, as he was known in the Italian press, greeted me warmly in Italian. Then he asked his assistant, Nina, to get us coffee and rejoin us. Nina was our translator.

Both were in buoyant moods. It was February 14, 2018, and on the previous day, Pope Francis had signed a decree recognizing a miracle attributed to the intercession of Blessed John Henry Newman, a nineteenth-century English cardinal, clearing the way for his canonization. The pope also recognized that the late Cardinal József Mindszenty, a Hungarian jailed and exiled by the Communists, had lived the Christian virtues in a heroic way and earned the designation as a Venerable. Ambrosi represented both causes and, in Newman's case, was credited with first reviving a difficult cause and now carrying it over the finish line. Newman was an Anglican priest who disagreed with his bishops enough that he joined the Catholic Church at the age of forty-four and was ordained a Catholic priest in 1846. He was a theologian, poet, and educator who prioritized making church teachings accessible for laypeople—he is the patron saint of Catholic campus ministries, and Newman Centers are a staple of public universities.

Newman's cause for sainthood was first opened in 1958, but it lost momentum when miracles attributed to him failed to materialize. His cause landed on Ambrosi's desk in the late 1990s. In 2009, Newman was beatified, or Blessed, on the strength of a healing miracle Ambrosi found in 2000. In Boston, Massachusetts, a man named Jack Sullivan was halfway through a four-year course to become a deacon—the level below priesthood in Catholic ministry—when brutal back pain nearly crippled him. One night, awaiting surgery to avoid paralysis, Sullivan watched a television show about Newman and his teachings. At the end of the show, a request appeared on-screen: viewers who received any divine favors were asked to contact the Birmingham Oratory, which was championing his cause. Sullivan wrote the information down and then prayed to Newman that he might walk pain-free so that he could finish his deacon class and be ordained.

When Sullivan awoke the next morning, the pain was gone.

A second miracle, the Saint-making one, happened in 2013 when an expectant mother in Chicago, Melissa Villalobos, was bleeding incessantly, threatening her un-born child's life. She prayed to Newman to intercede for her and her child. The bleeding stopped immediately. Her child was born perfectly healthy. She was healed completely.

What makes Ambrosi a successful miracle hunter is his knack for self-promotion, his loyalty to a certain strategy or playbook, and his genuine enthusiasm for the job. For over forty years, Ambrosi, seventy-one, has been perhaps the top postulator in the world. The red-covered vol-umes that are on his shelves and stacked on his furniture are just some of the six hundred causes that he says he has worked on. Twenty-two of them have become saints, such as Pope John XXIII (1881–1963), who opened the Second Vatican Council that put the Catholic Church in better sync with the modern world. Another dozen of his causes have been beatified and are one more miracle away from canonization. Among them is Emperor Charles I, the last emperor of the Austro-Hungarian Empire, who died in 1922 at the age of thirty-four. He was a peacemaker during World War I and let God's will inform his political decisions. Dozens more have been named Venerable, as Cardinal Mindszenty just had. Ambrosi had another thirty or forty causes in different stages that he currently was working on.

"I choose my causes carefully," Ambrosi said. "I need to convince myself that this person genuinely lived a holy life. If there is any artificiality, I turn it down."

In Ambrosi's telling, he was born into this business. His family's roots in Rome were planted centuries ago. His father, Alvaro, was a government administrator. His mother, Giovanna, stayed home and ran the family. Both were devout Catholics who made sure their family spent Sunday morning at Mass and their afternoons around the table listening to an uncle, a monsignor, tell stories about the interworkings of the Vatican. The Marianist priests taught him in grade school, and the Lasallian Brothers took over his education in high school. Ambrosi decided early on in life that he wanted to be a lawyer, the kind his uncle said worked behind the walls of the Vatican.

He earned a doctorate degree in civil law as well as canon law at the Pontifical Lateran University in Rome, which was founded in 1773 by Pope Clement XIV to teach theology and philosophy to seminarians from the Roman Colleges. It is informally known as the Pope's University because four of its graduates have been canonized, including Pope John Paul II.

In 1971, when Ambrosi was twenty-four, he took an unpaid internship in the Congregation for the Causes of Saints and has been part of its machinery ever since. At the time, anyone who wanted to get in the Saint-making business had to train at the congregation. Ambrosi was assigned to the office of Promoter of the Faith. Its official Latin title, *advocatus diaboli*, means devil's advocate. At the time, the Promoter of the Faith was a Spanish monk named Father Rafael Perez, who, with the assistance of four canon lawyers, shared an office above St. Peter's Square. They spent their days trying to pick apart the causes of would-be saints, whose arguments for divine sanctity inside the red volumes were stacked up in every corner.

Three days a week for three years, Ambrosi pored through causes looking for flaws in individual *positios* or miracle presentations—conflicting testimony from witnesses, unconvincing medical information that accompanied proposed miracles, anything that reeked of inauthenticity or diminished the candidate's claims to heroic virtue or miraculous intervention. He vacuumed these facts up and then wrote concise, convincing briefs why this priest or nun or missionary was not really saint material. Ambrosi was good at finding flaws in causes. Father Perez, according to Ambrosi, was an exacting boss who performed what was a job designed to be antagonistic with exceeding good humor. The monk was also imbued with divine nobility.

"He impressed on us that this was a centuries-old process and we were there to make sure that all we did had to meet the highest standards of canon law. It was the office's duty to raise the doubts and any questions about a cause so the pope's jury of cardinals and bishops had everything they needed to judge whether a cause should proceed."

During the other two days a week, Ambrosi drew a salary from a pair of canon lawyers whose practice was promoting causes of saints. The knowledge he was absorbing behind what was essentially enemy lines helped him recognize and anticipate weaknesses in causes. My dad would have admired this hustle with a smile for "playing both sides of the street."

"To be a good defender, you need to be a good accuser," said Ambrosi.

On December 20, 1974, the training of Ambrosi was completed and a formal decree from Father Perez declared that he was qualified to promote saintly causes. Ambrosi hung out his own shingle and quickly established himself as a keen-eyed judge of what made for a successful cause, as well as a man who knew his way around the Vatican, especially in the halls that counted most for his clients: the Congregation for the Causes of Saints.

It was not until January 25, 1983, however, that Ambrosi hit pay dirt—thanks to Pope John Paul II's *Divinus Perfectionis Magister*, the document that eliminated the powers of the Promoter of the Faith and the devil's advocate model, and reduced the number of miracles required for sainthood from four to two. Pope John Paul II wanted more saints. He wanted to market the Catholic Church more aggressively. The reforms in the document were intended to speed up the process by making it more accessible and less costly to people around the world. Pope John Paul II took advantage of the mechanism he put in place: over his twenty-seven-year reign, he anointed 1,338 Blesseds and canonized 482 new saints. Pope John Paul II was a Saint maker extraordinaire who turned the Congregation for the Causes of Saints into a "saint factory."

In the process, the pope shifted the power dynamic of Saint-making, as well as a whole lot of wealth. John Paul II allowed laypeople to become postulators if they had the proper training. Up until then, only priests could be the face of the cause—collecting and examining the historical and theological research and presenting the case of potential saints. With his formal training in the Congregation of the Causes of Saints completed and his carefully tended relationships with Vatican decision-makers cemented, Ambrosi was in the right place at the right time to become a postulator and build a heavenly empire.

At first, Ambrosi worked out of his apartment, but as he picked up more causes he moved into this modest office on Via Tor Millina, which has been his nerve center for more than thirty years. He acknowledges that he has leveraged his relationships with Vatican officials.

"They know who I am," Ambrosi said with a smile when I asked him how often he speaks face-to-face with the cardinals and bishops in the congregation.

His friendship with Monsignor Sarno, the Brooklyn-born priest who has been a fixture in the Congregation for the Causes of Saints for decades, has yielded several causes from the United States—some of them high profile, such as Archbishop Fulton Sheen and Cardinal Terence Cooke, as well as Father Edward Flanagan, who founded Boys Town in 1917 in a run-down Victorian mansion in downtown Omaha, Nebraska. He accepted boys of every race, color, and creed, and he believed "there are no bad boys, only bad environment, bad training, bad example, and bad thinking." Spencer Tracy portrayed him in a 1938 movie, *Boys Town*, and won an Oscar for the role. The Hollywood star spent his entire acceptance speech praising the priest. Ambrosi had other American causes, like Father Kapaun, which were lesser known but possessed fascinating backstories and ample financial backing from their sponsors. His causes also included those of Father Patrick Peyton, an early televangelist who coined the phrase "A family that prays together stays together," and Father Nelson Baker, a Civil War veteran and successful businessman who joined the priesthood and founded well-run orphanages and homes for unwed mothers.

Ambrosi had satisfied customers in the United States. Like he had just done with Cardinal Newman, Ambrosi had resurrected what had been a lost cause of Théodore Guérin, the French American nun who founded the Sisters of Providence of Saint Mary-of-the-Woods, a congregation at Saint Mary-of-the-Woods, Indiana. Her cause was first opened in 1907, and the order had gone through eight postulators before Ambrosi came on board in 1992. Fourteen years and two miracles later, Pope Benedict XVI canonized her Saint Theodora on October 15, 2006. The most impressive testament to the skills Ambrosi possesses as a postulator was his reviving of a miracle attributed to Saint Theodora in 1908 that a previous postulator had deemed unworthy. In the hands of Ambrosi, however, the recovery of Sister Mary Theodosia Mug from breast cancer, nerve damage to her arms, and a stomach tumor the morning after praying at Guérin's crypt was a miracle that got Theodora beatified.

With Monsignor Sarno's endorsement and good word-of-mouth, Ambrosi is usually the first stop for American dioceses and religious orders that want to launch a cause for sainthood. He isn't cheap. His rates are so high that neither he nor his clients wanted to discuss them.

When asked how much he charges for a cause,

Ambrosi waved his hand and insisted that he was not expensive. He explained that he had to travel frequently to interview witnesses and meet with sponsors of the cause, that there was a lot of research and writing involved, as well as hundreds upon thousands of documents that needed to be printed. Billable hours piled up. If I had learned anything about the Saint-making process, it was that it was a trial conducted by paper. Lots of it. Neither Ambrosi nor any other postulator got into the room during deliberations with the theologians or historians or cardinals and bishops to argue their sides.

"*Si*, expenses add up," he said with a shrug. "But when I have been in the United States and met with attorneys who work on different cases, and they tell me what their fees are, I was surprised that they make more in a day than I do in a month."

The Pontifical Commission for Reference on the Organization of the Economic-Administrative Structure of the Holy See saw it differently. Five months after being named pope, Francis set up this commission—with its titanic title—to examine, investigate, and ultimately reform how the Vatican did business. He wanted to reorganize a multibillion-dollar empire to ensure transparency, simplicity, and the efficient use of resources; and to be certain that the Church's mission of evangelization, especially for the poor and the marginalized, was being followed.

The commission's first stop was the Congregation for

the Causes of Saints, and what it found would be just the tip of the iceberg of waste and corruption within the vast network of Vatican finances. When the commission asked its Saint-making wing for financial records, they were told that none existed, according to internal documents given to Italian journalists Gianluigi Nuzzi and Emiliano Fittipaldi in 2012 that were part of what came to be known as Vatileaks. In 1983, Pope John Paul II ordered that funds for causes be managed by postulators, who had the "duty to keep regularly-updated ledgers on the capital, value, interests, and money in the coffers for every single cause," Nuzzi writes in his book *Merchants in the Temple: Inside Pope Francis's Secret Battle Against Corruption in the Vatican*.

No one, apparently, had heeded that command.

One of the casualties of this lack of oversight was the stunted growth in the Fund for the Causes of the Poor. The Holy See required that a portion of the leftover funds from a beatification or canonization be donated to the Fund for the Causes of the Poor. This fund was supposed to make it easier for poorer parts of the world to promote their own saints. Instead, the commission found that the Congregation for the Causes of Saints had failed to "fulfil this obligation" over the years to the extent that the fund had grown in a "very limited manner," according to the documents obtained by Nuzzi.

Between the volume of causes set in motion by Pope John Paul II and the escalating cost of mounting a

Saint bid, how and why were tens of millions of dollars unaccounted for?

The cost of opening a cause is about $55,000, with an additional $16,000 required for operating costs. This covers the compensation of the historian, theologians, physicians, and bishops who examine the cause. Once postulators go to work, however, the meter starts running—fast and skyward. The average cost of a cause is $550,000, though some can run as high as $1 million. Joseph Zahra, an economist from Malta who was heading the commission, zeroed in on the postulators, especially on Ambrosi and another lay postulator, Silvia Correale. Of the twenty-five hundred causes promoted by 450 different postulators, Ambrosi and Correale were disproportionately involved. Each had ninety cases, according to a commission report, versus the five or six causes, on average, handled by their colleagues. It meant that the two had a steady stream of revenues flowing in from dioceses and religious orders who often tapped their parishioners and supporters to donate to the causes of the saints that they were promoting.

Nuzzi, quoting the commission report, said that from 2008 to 2013, $51,000 was spent on a canonization that failed to make progress and offered no accounting on how the funds were used. One lay postulator asked for a $44,000 up-front payment to investigate the merits of a cause even before opening it. The commission report also made note that a printing shop owned by the

Ambrosi family—Novas Res—was one of three shops that the Congregation for the Causes of Saints recommended to postulators when they were putting together the hefty bound volumes that were then handed out to experts for study and to sponsors as keepsakes.

On Monday, August 5, 2013, Zahra ordered all bank accounts connected to beatification or canonization frozen: a total of nearly $45 million. Ambrosi had $1 million in three Vatican accounts that were locked up. In December 2013, the commission unblocked 114 of the 409 accounts it had blocked. Ambrosi's accounts were not among them. Instead, he was put on a stipend, Nuzzi writes, for months while the commission investigated.

Eventually, the restrictions were lifted and Ambrosi was very much back in business. He said that he continued to pick up American causes and pointed to some stairstep-sized *positios* that he had produced. He was aware of Pope Benedict XVI's mandate for brevity— if you call five hundred pages brief—but grew solemn when asked if he is writing shorter now.

"No, these are people with extraordinary lives, and you have to capture it all," he said. "Sometimes, it takes volumes. You can't leave anything out."

Ambrosi perked up, however, when I asked him to tell the story about how he became known as Dr. Ambrosi. He smiled and leaned up in his chair.

"When I first started investigating miracles, I'd go see the doctors and they didn't want to talk to me. I was a lawyer and they thought they were in trouble," he said. "I thought—I have a doctorate. If I put that in front of my name, they will be at ease, believing we share a profession."

My time was running out—his enthusiasm for our interview waned as my questions about his business practices and history probed a little too far for him. But I did need to know where the cause of Father Kapaun stood. Ambrosi caught a second wind and offered a soliloquy on the efforts of the Diocese of Wichita and especially Father Hotze's efforts to make Father Kapaun if not exactly a household name, one that resonated beyond the middle of America.

"It is not enough to have a virtuous candidate for sainthood, people have to know him, be devoted to him, to see themselves in him," he said.

To that end, Father Hotze and his team of volunteers had mounted an impressive ground game on behalf of Father Kapaun and his bid for sainthood. President Obama awarding him the Medal of Honor had reignited interest in his battlefield heroics. The Father Kapaun Guild, the infrastructure created to promote his cause, had sent prayer cards to all fifty states and dozens of countries. There were chapels named for the priest in Seoul, South Korea; Oiso, Japan; US Army Camp McGovern in Bosnia; and Kaiserslautern, Germany. There were memorials for Father Kapaun throughout Kansas and the Midwest and as far away as Honolulu, Hawaii.

Hundreds walked the sixty miles from Wichita to Pilsen each summer on a pilgrimage designed not only to remember Father Kapaun but as a spiritual exercise for all to find their pathway to sainthood—or at least a better spiritual life.

Membership in Kapaun's Men has swelled to more than one thousand. The group's mission was set out in a "Who We Are" section of a sophisticated website that streams highly produced videos of the virtues, the beatitudes, and stewardship. The group produces a *Call from the Foxhole* podcast series that features conversations with theologians and military chaplains, as well as Catholic bishops and priests. They offer a call-in number to pray a Sunday Rosary with fellow Kapaun devotees.

"Taking as our model the life of Father Emil Kapaun, a heroic Catholic priest and Army chaplain, Kapaun's Men are men who are committed to fighting the great spiritual battle that rages around us," reads the group's mission statement. "We are a band of brothers who do not fight alone. Jesus Christ is our strength and our leader. Father Kapaun is our friend and guide. A true Servant Leader, Father Kapaun epitomized Christian manhood and challenged his men to do the same. We desire to emulate his virtues and so become better husbands, fathers, leaders and friends."

The Father Kapaun Guild has a website that curates some of his letters and homilies and photographs. It solicits donations and sells items ranging from "Father

Kapaun Pray for Us!" bumper stickers ($2.50), a refrigerator magnet ($2.50), Chaplain Kapaun dog tags ($5.00), note cards ($7), to T-shirts and sweatshirts ($14 to $20), as well as medals and rosaries ($1 to $48). The tchotchkes are intended to build the brand of Father Kapaun and reach more people who might become devoted to him. They also raise money to offset a Saint campaign that has already cost more than $500,000—a significant portion of it going to the man sitting across from me.

"The fact that you are here to write a book about Father Kapaun proves how many people his life and virtue has touched," Ambrosi said.

Father Hotze had done his job. Ambrosi was doing his. He told me that the historians and theologians had given it their imprimatur with little resistance. Now it was a matter of getting on the schedule of the cardinals and bishops so they could decide if he could be declared Venerable. From there, the cause could proceed. He hoped that might happen before the end of the year, but it could be a year or two from happening. Ambrosi was pleased with the miracle Father Hotze had already surfaced in Kansas—that of Chase Kear, the junior college pole vaulter. His accident and miraculous recovery had been documented and vetted by American medical experts. It was ready to go.

"It is a shorter, more exact document," Ambrosi said. "We will submit it for inspection as soon as Father Kapaun is recognized for his heroic virtue."

What could stand in its way, I asked? That he was American, a region not considered a high priority? The fact that he was a military man? Or that he was a priest?

Ambrosi knew what I was getting at. I had timed my trip to Rome to coincide with the summit Pope Francis had called here to address the Catholic Church's "protection of minors." Every bishops' conference around the world was in Rome, an acknowledgment at the highest levels that the clergy sexual abuse, which exploded first in the United States, was a global problem. It was a first-of-its-kind gathering and had been announced the previous year, in September 2018, after abuse by priests became public in Ireland, Australia, Chile, Germany, Belgium, Canada, Italy, and Asia. In the United States, there seemed to be no end in sight. In August 2018, a Pennsylvania grand jury dropped a thirteen-hundred-page report that listed three hundred priests accused of the molestation of more than a thousand children in six of the state's eight dioceses over a seventy-year period.

Ambrosi grimaced. He nodded, yes, that may be a problem in light of the suspicious way American priests were currently viewed. He knew the late Bernard Francis Law, the cardinal and archbishop of Boston from 1984 until his resignation on December 13, 2002. Cardinal Law was forced out of Boston after church documents showed that he had extensive knowledge of sexual abuse committed by dozens of Catholic priests within his archdiocese and had failed to remove them from the ministry. When what happened in Boston came to light, it seemed like a tidal wave of similar abuse and cover-ups became public across the United States, and now the world. It was business as usual, a dirty business, that so far has resulted in the Church paying more than $3 billion in settlements in the United States alone. It tainted, and will continue to taint, priests among the faithful as well as the public at large.

The lawyer in Ambrosi, and devoted Catholic, questioned how the Church had handled the fallout. He said he was certain that they were credible cases.

"But maybe the Church should have defended itself?" he said.

Then abruptly, Ambrosi cut himself off. Instead, he smiled and, with the enthusiasm of a personal injury attorney passing his card out in an emergency room, asked:

"How about journalists?" he asked. "Is there any one of you who have led such extraordinary and virtuous lives that they might make a good cause to become a saint?"

14

Robert McGreevy was the first person ever to pray directly to Father Kapaun. He did so while standing on the dirt floor of the Death House in the prison camp at Pyoktong, Korea. He was dying and offered a plaintive plea to his departed friend.

"Father Kapaun, help me," he said.

That petition immediately brought him to his knees, then back to his feet. McGreevy found strength. He found the will to live, eventually becoming the rare prisoner to walk out of the Death House. He continued to say a daily prayer to Father Kapaun, even after he returned to his hometown of Cumberland, Maryland. He has prayed to his friend every day. He stopped going to Mass, however, years ago, sickened by the sexual abuse scandals that have soiled the Catholic Church in the United States. Instead, he bought a replica of the statue of Father Kapaun that stands in Pilsen, Kansas. It sits in his living room, surrounded by prayer cards, like the ones that were tucked into the bathroom mirror in the Hotze household, and in the homes of rural Kansans since the mid-1950s.

Like the ones that now circulate around the world requesting his intercession in language as plainspoken as the man himself.

Father Emil Kapaun gave
glory to God by following
his call to the priesthood and
thus serving the people of Kansas
and those in the military.
Father Kapaun, I ask your
intercession not only for these needs
which I mention now . . . but that I
too may follow your example of
service to God and my neighbor.
For the gifts of courage in battle
and perseverance of faith,
we give you thanks O Lord.

McGreevy prays to this makeshift shrine. Father Kapaun is his pastor just as he was when he was a nineteen-year-old soldier in a Korean prison camp. It is hard for him, and many of us, to reconcile a priest like Father Kapaun—a man who imitated the life of Christ—and the thousands of priests who have taken advantage of boys and girls—children—in the United States and beyond. It has been the elephant in the room for several generations of Americans, but one that no one dared talk about until early this century, after the *Boston Globe* detailed the abuses of its hometown diocese. Shortly before Pope Francis called the meeting on the protection of minors, I received a letter from my Jesuit high school with a list of priests who had served there over the decades and who faced allegations. It was part of a nationwide and long-overdue effort by the Jesuits to be transparent. The letter from my high school listed six individuals, and among them was the principal for all four of my years. There have been plenty of familiar names of parish priests who have made the pages of the *Kansas City Star* for their crimes. I am certain other parochial and Jesuit-educated Catholics across the country have seen the names of priests they knew in newspaper accounts about sexual abuse and settlements.

How did it go on so long in silence? There are books written about that by far more knowledgeable people than me, but I'll offer a newspaper version. The priests were skilled predators and narcissists. They took advantage of the innocence of children. Adults did not have the bandwidth to understand how something so heinous could be done by people they looked up to, whom they confided in, and whose hands they had put their own spiritual life in.

No sum of money can make up for the countless broken lives this has left, and continues to leave, behind. The damage is not only to those involved. A trust was badly broken, and its consequences are felt daily. A friend of mine, Drew, wanted his son and daughter to receive the sacrament of confirmation. It is the third of seven sacraments, and it follows baptism and Holy Communion and finalizes your initiation into the Catholic Church. Because both of his kids attended public schools, Drew asked them to attend Confraternity of Christian Doctrine—commonly known as CCD—classes at their parish. His son, then fourteen, asked him why they wanted to stay in a religion where "priests rape kids."

On the Sunday following the Pennsylvania grand jury report in 2018, which listed the priests accused of the molestation, another friend and colleague, Naka Nathaniel, was so fed up and defeated that he stood up at Sunday Mass and interrupted his priest's homily. The priest briefly addressed the report and acknowledged that he was surprised that people showed up for the service in the wake of such awful allegations. He said the Church had to change but was eager to move on with his homily.

"I couldn't help myself. I stood up and yelled out: 'Father! How?'" said Nathaniel.

When the priest told him to write the nuncio, the pope's representative in the United States, Nathaniel did not let him off the hook. He told him it was an unsatisfactory answer and then pointed at his nine-year-old son who was seated in the pew beside him.

"How could I ever let him make his First Communion?" he asked.

The moment went viral and in a subsequent opinion piece in the *New York Times*, Nathaniel wrote about how much the Church had meant to him and how devastated he now was.

"I wouldn't exist without Catholicism. My parents' interracial marriage was condoned by their families because they shared the religion. I was an altar boy and attended Catholic school. I played church-organized youth sports, and I was an Eagle Scout in the parish troop," he wrote.

"I attended Mass regularly while in college. Later, working as a journalist, it was a big thrill to cover Pope John Paul II's visit to New York in 1995. My non-Catholic wife and I were married in Holy Spirit Catholic Church in San Antonio."

Now, Nathaniel is angry. He is angry that the Church did not protect the innocent. He is angry that the Church covered up the sexual abuses. Nathaniel wants scalps—all of them from the pope on down for allowing the abuses to continue and be covered up. He also is angry at fellow Catholics like me who are not in full revolt about the Church's tolerance and cover-up of the abuses. Those who aren't asking for resignations: our silence, he believes, makes us complicit.

On the recessional at the end of the Mass, the priest whom Nathaniel confronted, a Jesuit named Father Mark Horak, stopped at Nathaniel's pew and told his son that his dad was a good dad.

"You and I have no influence," the priest turned and said to Nathaniel.

Nathaniel thought it was an honest response but also a terribly depressing one. So, like McGreevy, he has informally left the Catholic Church. He hasn't abandoned his faith, just those in charge of its customs. Nathaniel occasionally attends Mass with his parents.

"My connection to the Church is now purely through them," he said. "I go with them because it's such an essential part of their identities."

Being Catholic is essential to my identity as well, and it is at the core of my character—for better or worse. It has informed the most important decisions of my life. Who my partner is. How I live my life. How to raise my son. Who I want him to be. Being Catholic has honed my sense of justice and charity. How I look at the world. How I make my way in it.

Like most journalists, especially those steeped in the Jesuit way of thinking, I know enough about the Church's history, teachings, and foibles to be, as the saying goes, dangerous. Institutions and their hierarchies are human and corruptible, and over the centuries the Catholic Church has repeatedly demonstrated that in the bloodiest and most jaw-dropping ways. One pope, Pope John

XII (955–964), was a murderer who had mistresses—one of them whose husband caught the pope in bed with his wife and killed him. Another, Pope Stephen VI (896–897), had his predecessor, Pope Formosus, who had been dead for months, exhumed. He dressed Formosus in papal robes and sat him on the throne to stand trial. When the predictable guilty verdict came in, his body was dragged through the streets of Rome and dumped in the Tiber River. Months later, Pope Stephen VI was strangled to death by an enemy. Then there was Pope Clement VII (1523–1534), who offended Charles V, the Holy Emperor of Rome and Archduke of Austria, and was imprisoned while Rome was sacked in 1527 by German Protestants alongside Spanish and Italian mercenaries. The Church has treated women badly. It has shunned its lesbian, gay, bisexual, and transgender members. It has been judgmental and unbending. Its history is chockful of lowlights, and the sexual abuse scandal is the latest and among the worst.

This was my first time in Rome, my first time taking in the Vatican with its history and opulence and its place in the world as a moral authority—no matter how shaky its current footing. There were moments when I was deeply moved and rooted in my Catholicism.

The tomb of Saint Peter beneath the altar in the basilica named for him was a catechism lesson come to life. I believe it was Sister Clara Marie who told us to remember that the Roman Catholic Church was one *true*

Church because we could trace our beginnings all the way back to Jesus Christ. Peter was the first Bishop of Rome—or pope—because in Matthew 16:18, Jesus told him: "And I tell you that you are Peter, and on this rock I will build my church, and the gates of Hades will not overcome it." There was his tomb, right there in front of me, with Peter not only at the center of this architectural wonder, but as the rock for a religion that has spread from one Savior and a handful of followers to one that now counts 1.2 billion people worldwide.

My breath was taken away and tears flowed when I beheld Michelangelo's *Pietà* for the first time. Mary holding the body of her son after Jesus's crucifixion. The Carrara marble looks illuminated by divine light. The heartbroken face of a young mother. Jesus slack in her arms. The worst part of his mission behind him; our salvation a couple of days away. It is little wonder that it is the only piece Michelangelo ever signed. He must have known that this was the one piece with which he was truly guided by the hand of God. He was okay being associated with perfection.

Despite the efforts of Pope Francis to make the finances of the Church more transparent, no one knows for sure how much money or value the Catholic Church possesses. Its investments are kept secret. The Church holds vast amounts of gold. The treasures in its museums have never been properly appraised; the same with its land holdings. The Vatican is one of the largest landowners in

Europe, with retail and apartment buildings from Italy to England, in France and Switzerland. Best-guess estimates are that the Catholic Church is worth anywhere from $10 to $15 billion. What is clear, however, is that the Catholic Church has too much money, wants to keep it (much of it right there in Rome), and prefers secrecy over a full accounting. Those factors in combination make the institution and its officials corruptible, and both have proven to be just that time and time again. It is why I prefer my friend Bob Berner's view that we the people are the Church.

Still, for four days in February 2019, Pope Francis summoned the presidents of many of the bishops' conferences of the world, men's and women's religious orders, and powerful cardinals—190 in all—to address the Church's sexual abuse problem. Each day, they watched videotaped testimony from abuse survivors, including a woman who at age fifteen was abused by a priest who got her pregnant three times and forced her to have abortions.

Still, sexual abuse survivors and their advocates did not expect any landmark changes to result. Indeed, there was so much resistance from the world's bishops that they could not even acknowledge that attention to the issue was critical—instead they suggested that cases were isolated and if there was a problem it was largely an American one. Some bishops claimed any abuse was the result of gay priests in the Church, an allegation that scientific studies had disproved. On the rare occasions that bishops did acknowledge abuse, they preferred to treat it as a sin to forgive, and not a crime.

It is hard for me to type those previous sentences.

It should be hard for you to read.

If the pope and his bishops needed any more reminders of the scope of this ongoing abuse and how close it was to Rome, it came the week before this gathering, when Francis defrocked an American cardinal, Theodore McCarrick. Over decades, McCarrick had been accused of improper sexual conduct with adult seminarians, and then in 2018, allegations of his abuse of minors surfaced. Two months earlier, Australian cardinal George Pell, once the Vatican's treasurer, was found guilty on five charges related to serious sexual misconduct involving two boys at St. Patrick's Cathedral in Melbourne in the 1990s.

Pope Francis had a mixed track record when it came to addressing allegations of abuse. In January of the previous year on a trip to South America, Pope Francis defended Bishop Juan Barros Madrid—whom he had appointed—against charges that the bishop protected a pedophile priest. Before celebrating Mass outside the northern Chilean city of Iquique, Pope Francis said the allegations against Barros were unfounded.

"The day someone brings me proof against Bishop Barros, then I will talk," Francis said. "But there is not one single piece of evidence. It is all slander. Is that clear?"

The anger and disappointment of Catholics in Chile was immediate and powerful enough for Pope Francis to reconsider his defense of Barros. He sent a sexual abuse investigator to the country to examine the allegations. In April 2018, after receiving a twenty-three-hundred-page report on the matter, Francis admitted making "serious mistakes" in his handling of sexual abuse cases in Chile. He also summoned abuse survivors from the country to the Vatican to hear their stories and offer his regrets. In May 2018, Chile's bishops traveled to Rome, where they all offered their resignations. The pope accepted five of them, including Barros, for covering up for the priests and dismissing victims' allegations, much as the pope had.

It was a woman, however, who challenged the Church's culture of silence on sexual issues at the summit. Sister Veronica Openibo, a Nigerian-born nun, criticized the practice of letting elderly clergy who had abused children disappear quietly with their pension and reputations intact.

"Let us not hide such events anymore because of the fear of making mistakes," she said. "Too often we want to keep silent until the storm has passed! This storm will not pass by. Our credibility is at stake."

She turned to Pope Francis, who shared the dais, and called for a policy of "zero tolerance" toward clergy who abuse children. Sister Openibo addressed him directly as Brother Francis and commended him for owning up to his mistakes in his handling of the sexual abuse cases in Chile. She chided him, too, for the fact that she was one of only a dozen women invited to the summit and one of only three women to speak before the group.

"Usually, it is just the men who come," Openibo said with a smile.

In closing, Sister Openibo said what the cardinals, bishops, and priests rarely do.

"Thank you for providing this opportunity for us to check and see where we have acted strangely, ignorantly, secretly, and complacently," she said.

In the end, however, it mattered little. Like with its finances, the Vatican prefers secrecy over a full accounting.

Yes, Pope Francis talked a good game.

"Consecrated persons, chosen by God to guide souls to salvation, let themselves be dominated by their human frailty or sickness and thus become tools of Satan," he said in his closing speech. "In abuse, we see the hand of the evil that does not spare even the innocence of children. No explanations suffice for these abuses involving children."

But he did not wield the big stick. He is the pope. He is infallible. What he says goes. Pope Francis could have installed that policy of zero tolerance. He could have mandated that priests with credible allegations be removed and their cases reported and turned over to authorities. Instead, he tried to win the hearts and minds of colleagues, many of whom do not even acknowledge that the sexual abuse allegations are a problem. He encouraged them to protect the children in their flock. He did not command them to do so. Like any kingdom, there is palace intrigue in the Vatican, and, as popular as Pope Francis is with the people whom he leads, he remains a divisive figure among his own hierarchy, especially among a large conservative wing that fear he is moving too fast to embrace the modern world with all its problems. His allies argued that if he took a hard line, he risked alienating the conservative-leaning faithful in Latin American, African, and Asian countries where the future of the Church lies. Instead, he was trying to persuade bishops to own the problem at the local level. Instead of dismissing allegations and covering up, the pope urged the bishops to be compassionate and accountable for protecting the innocent.

It was better for the brand. But was it better for its victims? Children today and in the future? For the Church? The survivors and their advocates sure did not believe so. Neither did Robert McGreevy nor Naka Nathaniel. I didn't, either. If ever an institution needed the gift of courage in battle, it was now. If ever the faithful needed the perseverance of faith, it was us.

"Father Kapaun, help them . . ."

"Father Kapaun, help us . . ."

"Father Kapaun, help me . . ."

15

Do you believe in miracles?

Not the kinds tossed around to describe sporting events like the "Miracle on Ice," as the US hockey team's victory over the Soviet Union at the 1980 Winter Olympics in Lake Placid, New York, is known. Not the miracles assigned daily to tasks like putting out a newspaper or catching a plane flight after enduring a harrowing traffic jam. Not even the profound-feeling miracles of life that wash over you, like when you first hold your newborn son or daughter.

No, I'm talking the real thing, like Jesus turning the water into wine or raising Lazarus from the dead. In the dictionary, a miracle is defined as a "surprising and welcome event that is not explicable by natural or scientific laws and is therefore considered to be the work of a divine agency." In fact, four out of five Americans do believe in miracles, according to a Pew Research poll, which shows well of our nation's soul and how spirituality has caught on.

Before the afternoon of October 2, 2008, however, Chase Kear had never had a reason to ponder miracles. He was a nineteen-year-old college athlete—a pole vaulter—who drank a little beer, dipped tobacco occasionally, and liked his radio tuned to a country-and-western station. He turned the dial up when he heard Kenny Chesney. He grew up in Colwich, Kansas, whose name is a mash-up for the Colorado-Wichita Railroad. It's a town that boasts a population of fourteen hundred people, many of whom work in Wichita, eighteen miles to the southeast. Chase won state championships as a member of Andale High School's football, wrestling, and track-and-field teams. In fact, he is the only student in school history to have achieved that trifecta. It was pole vaulting, however, that really got under his skin—because of the discipline and precision it demanded in order for him to take flight. It was his father's sport as well—Paul Kear was a pole vaulter at Fort Hays State University.

Chase was outgoing and gregarious with circles upon circles of friends—that happens in rural parts of the state when the same kids from the same kind of small towns compete against each other year after year. He stood five feet, ten inches tall and was broad shouldered. His arms and leg muscles looked like they were threaded with steel cable. He had thick sandy hair and was still tan from summer. He went to Mass on Sunday, but by no means was he devout.

At practice the day before, Chase had charged down the runway, pole in hand, hit the box perfectly, launched himself fifteen feet, seven inches into the air, and cleared the bar easily. It was the highest that he had ever vaulted and made him the winner of the informal competition between him and his teammates at Hutchinson Community College in Hutchinson, Kansas. He did it on the first day of practice in his sophomore year. He was certain that this was going to be a season to remember.

Now he was enjoying his bragging rights, talking some trash, and telling his teammates just how spectacular this season—his season—was going to be. One of them tried to put Chase back in his place, telling him that he would never be king of the vaulters in Hutchinson until he had broken a pole. Breaking a pole is sort of a rite of passage for pole vaulters—a badge of honor. It means you hit the box so powerfully and so perfectly that the pole snaps at the apex of the jump.

"So I found an old pole, one that I knew I could break, and rolled down the runway with purpose," Chase said. "I planted. I powered up. I cleared it."

On the way down, however, Chase got sideways. He twisted and tried to land on his back, but it just made his positioning worse. Instead, his butt hit the side of the mat and bounced him off it altogether. The back of

Chase's head smashed into the concrete. He saw the flash of white light. He had failed to break his pole, but when he put his hands to his head, Chase knew he had broken something badly. He felt his skull swivel and was stunned that he was able to spread it open. He had cracked it in half from ear to ear.

Then everything went dark.

His coach, Pat Becher, dialed Kear's parents as soon as their son was put on a helicopter and transported to Via Christi Regional Medical Center St. Francis in Wichita. Chase had stopped breathing and had to be intubated. His body was limp. His eyes remained open, but his eyeballs were floating in different directions.

"It's bad, it's really bad," Becher told Chase's mother, Paula Kear, over the phone. "He was vaulting, and he missed the mat."

By the time Paula and her husband, Paul, got to the hospital, the prognosis for their son was dire. Chase's head trauma was so severe, doctors told them, that if their son managed to live, it would not be much of a life at all.

"Institutions, diapers, a vegetable, I mean that's what we were facing," said Paula Kear.

The Kears asked the chaplain at the hospital to perform the sacrament of last rites. They were practicing Catholics who every morning gathered Chase and his two younger brothers, Cole and Clay, for a morning prayer. They repeated the ritual every night. They went to Mass on Sundays, getting to Sacred Heart church early enough to join the prayer line, a gathering of parishioners who offered prayers for each other's special intentions. It was Paula Kear's sister, Linda Wapelhorst, who called Sacred Heart and told them that Chase needed help. He needed so much help that she asked that they pray to Father Kapaun, considered in the parish to be the prayer of last resort for people suffering greatly and who were on their way out of this world. At the hospital, Paul and Paula had already put the priest's prayer card on their son's bed. His brothers, Cole and Clay, decided to go even wider: they posted the prayer for the intercession of Father Kapaun on a Facebook page and asked for prayers.

Chase's neurosurgeon, Dr. Raymond Grundmeyer, told the Kears that the only option was to immediately remove part of his skull. His brain was swelling rapidly, and if they removed part of his cranium, that swelling would have somewhere to go, relieving the pressure. It was risky, Dr. Grundmeyer told them. Chase might not make it off the table. If he did, there was a very likely chance that Chase could pick up an infection that would eventually kill him. The Kears told Grundmeyer to go ahead and do the surgery.

Then nothing.

Chase remained in a coma.

But the prayer line at Sacred Heart continued to hum. The crowds before daily Mass swelled and their voices lifted as they asked for the intercession of Father

Kapaun so Chase could have a full recovery. Online, Cole and Clay's Facebook page was getting thousands of clicks and comments from friends and strangers alike, some of them from as far away as Europe and Australia. Both Paul and Paula Kear are from big families with sixteen siblings between them and sixty-one cousins of Chase's generation. Some days, there were as many as one hundred family members and friends in the hospital waiting room, their lips murmuring the Father Kapaun prayer and their fingers working rosaries.

One, two, six days went by and Chase lay there as limp and as unresponsive as when he arrived. On the seventh day, Paul Kear leaned in close to his son and asked—pleaded—for Chase to give him a sign that he was fighting, that he might recover after all. A moment, another, and then another went by. Then Paul saw his son move his finger. Once. Twice.

"I don't remember it, but it was enough to let them know I was still in there," Chase said.

The nurses, however, warned Paul and Paula Kear not to read too much into the wagged finger. It could have been a reflex or spasm. Two days later, however, a nurse took Chase's hand and asked him to squeeze it if he could hear her. She felt a grip. His brain was working after all. Soon, Chase started recognizing Paul and Paula, Cole and Clay. Then words started to form—haltingly. When the nurses and doctors were convinced that Chase was cognizant, they moved him out of the intensive care unit

into a regular room. He had been clinging to life in the
ICU for seventeen days. Two days later, the most vivid
memory that Chase retains of the early days of his ordeal
came when the nurses stood him up next to his bed, a
hole as big as a baseball on the right side of the skull.
If he could stand on his own for seven seconds, he was
told, he would be moved to a hospital across town to
begin his rehabilitation.

Chase strained. He wobbled. He willed himself to
keep standing. He passed the test.

At Wesley Rehabilitation Hospital, Chase was known
as the miracle patient as soon as he arrived. His com-
petitiveness and athleticism were on display in the way
he attacked his exercises. He was, and remains, a self-
described "perfectionist." He had been a slight kid until
he started hitting the weight room in high school. It had
taken him three years to master the mechanics of pole
vaulting, an event that relies on technique and muscle
memory. Still, Chase never got discouraged. By his
senior year, he had willed himself to a third-place finish
in the Kansas state championships and earned a scholarship at Hutchinson Community College in the highly
competitive junior-college Jayhawk League.

Chase put the same type of effort into his rehabilitation at Wesley. He asked for extra exercises and stayed
at them longer. He wrestled down the math problems
given to him, rifled through the flash cards, and did his
memory exercises to sharpen and focus his traumatized

brain. Chase was the hospital's star student who mastered in days and weeks tasks that took other patients months and years to achieve. He was a marvel, especially considering that 10 percent of his brain had been removed, including one-third of the portion that governed his motor skills.

As hard as Chase was working at Wesley, his family and friends were matching that effort on the Father Kapaun prayer lines. His hospital room continued to be filled with friends and family in the little downtime that he had between rehabilitation sessions. The Kears did not have to shop or cook—food was being dropped off at their home. Carpools were ferrying Cole and Clay to their own sports practices. Their neighbors and friends held fundraisers to offset the Kears' medical bills.

Seven weeks after cracking his head open, seven weeks after he was supposed to be dead, Chase Kear walked out of the hospital and climbed into his parents' car. He pressed his nose against the window as a police escort slowly led him home to Colwich, where the streets were lined with neighbors and parishioners who waved and applauded with tears in their eyes. Chase's track teammates from Hutchinson had loaded onto a team bus and had driven the forty miles from school to be there. They were waiting on his driveway. Television cameras and reporters were in his yard.

Chase had lived these seven weeks in a bubble, a foggy one due to the nature of his injury. As he made his way to his door, between handshakes and hugs, Chase was shuddering. His heart was beating too fast. Tears were banging on the back of his eyes wanting to escape. The legs that he had worked so hard to steel were going rubbery.

"I had no idea," he said, "how many people were on my side. I had no idea how many had hit their knees and prayed to Father Kapaun. I was overwhelmed. I was lifted. I was just amazed, and I cried for most of the night."

Chase returned to Hutchinson Community College the following year where, as a twenty-year-old, he coached the pole vaulters. His life continued at a young man's velocity. From Hutchinson, Chase went to Fort Hays State University in Fort Hays, Kansas, where he continued to coach his sport for the track team and earned his bachelor's degree in communications. Chase even managed to go airborne again. He practiced a three-step approach to the pole vault box until he was finally able to clear a bar set much lower than his best. After what he had endured, it felt like a world-record jump to Chase.

For the cause of Father Kapaun, Chase's recovery was complete and permanent, which meets part of the criteria for validating a miracle. Permanent recovery is a must for the cause of any would-be saint. The second criterion is that his recovery defy medical explanation. His neurosurgeon, Dr. Grundmeyer, has attested, and

Dr. Ambrosi has written up, that there was not a scientific basis for his recovery. Other doctors involved in his case have agreed.

"He was on death's door," said Grundmeyer. "And I would have to say, from a religious perspective, in Chase's situation, with the background of his parents and family and friends, the spirituality there, and the fact that he's recovered so well—you almost have to believe that there's something additional going on than your typical medicine. This was definitely miraculous."

Together, if it is accepted as a miracle, Chase's recovery proves that not only is Father Kapaun in heaven with God but he is also in God's favor. The torrent of prayers—or intercessions—to Father Kapaun demonstrated this and prompted God to intervene and perform a miracle. Ultimately, a panel of doctors selected by the Vatican will decide if this is, indeed, true and affirm that Father Kapaun is worthy of beatification.

In the meantime, it took time for Chase, now thirty-one, to absorb what happened to him, why it happened, and what he was supposed to do next. He remains fuzzy on his seven weeks in the hospital. He does not know where he found the strength to endure and get stronger.

"I did a television interview in the hospital that I can't remember doing," said Chase. "I was out of it for most of those weeks."

However, it did not take Chase long to discover how hard it was to be a living miracle. The nickname Miracle

Man stuck with him for several years after his recovery. It echoed behind him in The Keg, Colwich's local bar and grill, whenever he stopped in for a burger and beer. At both Hutchinson and Fort Hays State, Chase was approached by acquaintances and strangers who wanted to touch him. They asked probing questions, wanting to understand if he, indeed, believed that he was on the receiving end of a miracle. Many times, it made for uncomfortable conversations.

Like many college graduates, Chase drifted from job to job—among them selling guns from the sporting goods department at a Walmart—not certain what he wanted to do with his life. There was a broken heart to overcome. Chase had a girlfriend at the time of his accident who subsequently became his fiancé. About four months after he left the hospital, they broke up. Beyond the arced scar on the right side of his head and the ceramic plate in his head, there also are everyday reminders of his accident.

"My memory is scrambled, so I have to do little tricks to remember things. It's not noticeable to anyone," Chase said. "Like when I meet someone, I'm looking at them and saying their name to myself dozens or even hundreds of times so I will remember them. It's my battle, one that I fight every day."

Sometimes, Chase says that he was his own worst enemy. Those perfectionist tendencies that he relied on to push himself—to become a hard-hitting football

player, a fierce wrestler, a technically adept pole vaulter—
became an obstacle in understanding what had happened
to him. He got impatient and became frustrated when he
was struggling to find his purpose in life.

"For so long, I had to be better today than I was
yesterday," he said. "They say God has a plan for everyone. What's the plan? I wanted to know so badly so I
wouldn't screw it up."

Finally, Chase decided that he had to let go. He
quit asking, Why me? Instead, he accepted that he was
supposed to be dead. He accepted that he was missing
part of his brain and that those everyday battles with his
memory were a gift. Chase decided not to get uncomfortable anymore when people wanted to touch a miracle
or at least talk to him about it, to try to understand. He
spoke with reporters and appeared on network or religious television shows. The more that he talked about
his journey, the better he accepted it. He prayed more
often. He listened to what God was telling his heart.
Chase replaced impatience with gratitude.

"It finally clicked with me that it was not supposed to be
possible that you and I are talking," Chase said. "I was not
supposed to walk out of that hospital. I was supposed to
die on the operating table or in a bed. Or worse—still be
alive but brain-dead. But I'm not, because of the prayers
of people I know, and the prayers of people I will never
know, to a priest who lived a saintly life. I was given a second chance. I was given a chance to hit the reset button."

When Chase let go and let God in, he found peace. He found it in his art—he draws and paints, and carries and points a thirty-five-millimeter camera. He is even more involved in pole vaulting, coaching the discipline at high schools in Wichita. He found more than a job; he found a career at an aviation company with defense contracts that builds airplane engines.

So, does he think Father Kapaun should be a saint? Is his miracle enough to move the priest closer to canonization?

Chase told me a story about how he had attended the Medal of Honor ceremony for Father Kapaun in the East Room of the White House. He met the nine prisoners of war who had served with the priest. He told me how he was overcome with their devotion to Father Kapaun. Among them was Herb Miller, the wounded soldier the priest first saved from being shot and then carried to the prison camp and helped keep alive while there. Chase saw himself in Miller.

"Just like he carried him, Father Kapaun has carried me," he said. "All those guys who knew him said he was a living saint. I am with them. If my miracle helps make it official—great. But he is always going to be a saint to me."

16

Avery Gerleman has a tattoo etched below her right rib cage near the scar where her chest was cracked open in surgery. It is two words from the Gospel of St. Mark: *talitha koum*. In Aramaic, it means "little girl, arise" and was spoken by Jesus to a twelve-year-old girl who'd lain before him dead. The girl rose. For eighty-seven days, Avery's father, Shawn, spoke those words frequently as he sat in a recliner beside the hospital bed of his twelve-year-old daughter.

Their saga, their miraculous journey, begins on a soccer field in Fayetteville, Arkansas, in October 2006. Avery had just scored a goal for her team, the Wichita Attack, when she sprinted to the sidelines and spit up blood. Avery's mother, Melissa Gerleman, took her to a local emergency room, where her daughter was diagnosed with pneumonia. The Gerlemans headed home to Wichita, but Avery was barely conscious and

211

still coughing up blood, so Melissa took her straight to Wesley Medical Center. Doctors there admitted her and treated her for dehydration. For four days, Avery lay in a hospital bed not really getting any better.

It was a respiratory therapist who recognized that Avery was in trouble. She noticed Avery was having trouble breathing and feared that her lungs may be damaged. It was a call to arms for the doctors and nurses caring for her. Suddenly, new machines were wheeled in and out of her room to perform more tests on her lungs, her kidneys, her liver. When Avery still struggled to breathe, she was put on a ventilator. Her kidneys were failing. Her blood vessels were disintegrating. Each new test failed to yield answers. Shawn and Melissa tried to reassure their daughter that the doctors were going to figure out what was wrong and make her feel better.

Avery was not so sure. With a tube down her throat, she picked up a pad and paper and wrote a note to her parents.

"Am I going to die?" it read.

Shawn and Melissa were praying for their daughter's recovery, but the doctors were not giving them much encouragement. Avery's two main doctors, Michelle Hilgenfeld and Lindall Smith, were stymied. Dr. Hilgenfeld, a nephrologist, was focused on Avery's kidneys. They were failing and she did not know why. Dr. Smith, an experienced pediatric intensive care physician, was alarmed by the breakdown of Avery's other vital organs.

The doctors had induced Avery into a coma to buy some time, and they put her on a dialysis machine to keep her kidneys working. Smith convened an all-hands-on-deck meeting of his colleagues—about twenty in all—to brainstorm and go through medical books to match Avery's symptoms to a disease.

When Melissa asked Dr. Smith if there was anything he could do, the doctor suggested perhaps transferring Avery to a colleague and specialist in a nearby state. Suddenly, however, he reconsidered.

"I don't think she could survive the flight," Dr. Smith told Shawn and Melissa. "There's not a lot more we can do for her."

Melissa collapsed into her husband's arms.

"She will live," Shawn answered back.

Shawn and Melissa prayed. Shawn was a believer in intercessory prayer—asking someone you know who is in heaven to pray for you. Each week for an hour, Shawn went to the chapel at St. Patrick Catholic Church, his parish, to pray and think. He had incorporated intercessory praying into his devotional routine. Sometimes, he prayed to saints. Often, he prayed to his deceased grandfather. In fact, it was after his grandfather's death that he was introduced to Father Kapaun. Shawn discovered a dusty old copy of a book on the priest that was published by the Didde Catholic Campus Center at Emporia State University in his hometown, Emporia, Kansas. His grandmother had worked there, as had Shawn, for two years as a development director helping the center raise money.

Shawn took the book home and read it in one sitting. The story of Father Kapaun, and especially his courage, resonated with him. In fact, Shawn had passed on his admiration for the priest to Avery so enthusiastically that she asked her second-grade teacher at the Catholic school she attended if she could write about Father Kapaun. The assignment was to write a paper on a saint, which the priest was not. In fact, his cause for sainthood was just being put together. No matter—Avery was granted permission and her paper received an A+ grade. Avery's final words of the three-page paper were prophetic: "Chaplain Kapaun, pray for us."

Avery's fascination with Father Kapaun was deep. One day, Melissa and Avery—all of seven years old—were at the grocery store, and she chattered on about Father Kapaun.

"He is a good man," Avery said. "He's a good man."

Early in his daughter's hospital stay, Shawn remembered the paper and Avery's fondness for the late priest, so he began writing prayers to Father Kapaun. Shawn carried a notebook with him at the hospital, primarily to keep track of the doctors' diagnoses and the medications Avery was receiving. But as Shawn's written prayers piled up in its pages, that notebook evolved into a prayer book and, finally, a more than one-hundred-page diary of hope.

"Fr. Kapaun. Take all the prayers said for Avery this week & lay them at the feet of the Lord. Intercede & obtain a miracle for Avery, full & immediate recovery for the Greater Glory of God," Shawn wrote on October 28.

The Gerlemans were active in their parish and soon the prayers were echoing within the walls of St. Patrick's for their daughter, a fierce young athlete who looked nothing like the young person now motionless in a hospital bed and attached to several machines. Tubes were laced through her. The *thump, thump, thump* of a dialysis machine filled her room. Avery's face was bloated and skin infections had erupted all over her body.

Shawn or Melissa stayed with her around the clock. Shawn, an insurance man, took the night shift. Melissa, a special education teacher, had taken a leave so she could be there all day. They held Avery's hand. They told her what Haley, her older sister, was doing in school. They talked to her about vacations they'd taken, highlights of soccer games, and other moments of triumph in their little girl's life. They cried. Shawn, at night in the recliner with a blanket pulled over his head, and Melissa during the days. She would find a corner of the room away from the nurses as one medical crisis after another threatened to take Avery.

The latest one had to do with Avery's heart. The sac that surrounded the heart had filled with fluid and threatened to strangle it. Dr. Smith called for a surgeon in the hopes of draining the sac and relieving the pressure on Avery's heart. The problem was Avery was too weak to be moved into an operating room. Her condition was so fragile that Dr. Smith believed moving Avery even a few floors and preparing her for surgery would be fatal. Instead, he asked the surgeon to open up Avery and drain her sac right there in her room.

The surgeon was aghast.

"I don't know why you are even considering this," the surgeon said. "She's not going to make it, no matter what we do."

Unbeknownst to the surgeon, Melissa had slipped into the room and heard what he had said. She had kept her composure for weeks as the doctors told her about one problem after another Avery was facing. She had remained hopeful. Not this time—to hear the surgeon pronounce a death sentence on her daughter was too much. She shook. She sobbed. Dr. Smith sidled the surgeon over to the side of the room. He showed him some lab reports. Dr. Smith agreed with him that cracking open her chest to drain fluid from her heart and stomach was risky. But he had little other choice. Dr. Smith was not ready to give up on Avery and neither were her parents. It had to be done. The surgeon relented. Avery's room was made as sterile as possible, and the surgeon opened her up right there in bed and drained the fluids that were threatening her heart. Avery had escaped again.

Shawn's diary had a new entry: "Fr. Kapaun, take the

petition to the Lord. Lord, forgive me for being selfish. I want a miracle healing."

Avery's thirteenth birthday on October 31 passed without a celebration. The next day, however, the pastor at Saint Patrick's, Father Eric Weldon, decided to turn up the prayer volume for Avery. It was All Saints' Day and Father Weldon made an announcement at each Mass that Avery was in dire shape and needed their prayers for a recovery. They needed to pray to Father Kapaun.

At Wesley Medical Center, Dr. Hilgenfeld finally found a disease that fit Avery's symptoms: pulmonary renal syndrome, an autoimmune disorder that disarms the body's defense system. Viruses and toxins were going unchecked, and Avery's antibodies were bombarding her blood vessels and damaging every organ with which they came in contact. There was a course of treatment available: therapeutic plasma exchange. It sounded space-age, but really it was a way of putting blood through a filter. Avery's blood would be spun in a centrifuge where the healthy blood cells and platelets would be separated from the plasma. Then the bad plasma would be replaced, and the healthy cells and platelets and working antibodies would be put back into Avery's body. It was a nerve-racking procedure that could last up to four grueling hours.

Still, Shawn and Melissa refused to lose hope. They continued to whisper *"Talitha koum"* to their daughter. They continued to pray to Father Kapaun.

"I ask Fr. Kapaun. I recognize his compassion for sick and injured & I ask him to present my petitions to Lord for the perfect healing of lungs & kidneys. I add—make this disease go away. Heal her, Lord," Shawn wrote in his journal at 4:20 a.m. on November 4.

Each day, Shawn and Melissa stepped around the dozen or so medical devices in Avery's hospital room that were keeping her breathing and fighting her infections. They reached through the tubes looping around her like a halo to rub and flex her muscles. They gave her sponge baths to maintain her dignity. The doctors believed the plasma replacement may have slowed the deterioration of her organs, but none of them believed Avery was going to survive.

Shawn and Melissa did.

Sixteen days after the people of St. Patrick's prayed for Avery, Dr. Smith decided it was time for Avery to come off the ventilator. He lowered the amount of sedative that she was receiving to bring her out of the coma. Dr. Smith was not sure Avery could breathe on her own. He was afraid that she had not been able to receive enough oxygen to keep her brain working at all.

He was braced for the worst. When he pulled the tube out, however, Avery gasped and then the breaths came one after another—first in a rush, then settling into an easy rhythm. Next, Avery's eyelids flickered and then opened altogether. She saw Shawn and Melissa, and the brightness in her eyes showed that she recognized them.

Her mouth opened to form words that could not yet come. The following day, however, Avery was talking to her parents. Two days after that, Avery's kidneys started to work on their own.

On November 23, 2006, Thanksgiving Day, Dr. Hilgenfeld offered a smile and a look of wonder to Shawn and Melissa.

"If someone does not know God, introduce them to Avery Gerleman," she told them.

Two days later, on November 25, Avery watched her favorite college basketball team, the Kansas Jayhawks, play Florida. Or at least part of it—she drifted off to sleep before halftime.

Each day, a different tube seemed to come out of Avery, or a medicine was reduced or eliminated altogether. She had lost thirty pounds and, at sixty-six pounds and bone-thin, she could easily be lifted from her bed. Avery started eating though—first soup and crackers, then eggs and toast, and eventually hospital blue-plates with ice cream. On December 4, 2006, braced by two physical therapists, Avery stood beside her bed. The pain was almost unbearable, but that was not why she was crying. It was not why Shawn and Melissa were sobbing, either.

Little girl had arisen.

On January 2, 2007, Avery walked out of Wesley Medical Center to the amazement of Dr. Smith and Dr. Hilgenfeld. They were certain she would not live, or, if she did manage to survive, would require dialysis and oxygen for the rest of her life. No one's lungs and kidneys could absorb the amount of trauma Avery's had and continue to function. They told this to Shawn and Melissa because they wanted them to be as prepared as possible for a grim outcome. Instead, X-rays showed Avery's kidneys and lungs were in pristine condition. No scarring or tissue damage.

Six months later, Shawn, Melissa, and Avery had a follow-up appointment with Dr. Hilgenfeld. Again, the doctor was surprised at what she saw—Avery was in perfect health. She was as well and as smiley and as happy as any thirteen-year-old set loose in the world. When Avery told her that she was back on the youth soccer fields and scoring goals, the doctor was in awe.

"Quite honestly, Avery should have not left the hospital alive," she told them.

No more follow-up visits were ever required.

Unlike Chase Kear, Avery picked up her life untroubled. She played soccer in high school well enough to earn an athletic scholarship at Hutchinson Community College in Hutchinson, Kansas, and, like Chase, earned her associate's degree there. She does not remember much of her eighty-seven days near death in the Wesley Medical Center. But miracle or not, the experience gave her direction. Avery decided that she was put on earth to help the suffering and sick. So she became a nurse, earning her licensed practical nurse license at Wichita Area Technical College in 2016. Her first job? A nursing assistant at Wesley Medical Center in the same pediatric intensive care unit where she was treated, and alongside Dr. Smith and Dr. Hilgenfeld and many of the same nurses who had cared for her.

"It was something I felt pulled to do," Avery said. "I really can't remember the medical ups and downs, but I do remember how kind and caring the nurses were. When you're a kid and scared and hurting, that's worth a lot."

Now twenty-six, after a five-year stint at Wesley Medical Center, Avery recently followed Shawn and Melissa from Wichita to Emporia. She has been working in a doctor's office and preparing to return to school to pursue a registered nurse degree. Shawn and Melissa, frankly, were surprised but pleased that their youngest daughter uprooted her life to be close to them.

Avery said that they should not be.

"I am where I am because of my faith and family," she said.

There is no doubt in Avery's mind that her recovery was a miracle and that Father Kapaun interceded on her behalf. She told Andrea Ambrosi so when he came to Wichita in 2009. She and her parents spent a long lunch with the postulator for Father Kapaun, telling him the story of her sudden illness and recovery. She gave him the paper she wrote about the priest in the second grade. Shawn handed over his journal. Dr. Smith and Dr. Hilgenfeld met with him as well, and they assured him that there was no medical explanation for her to have survived. Neither doctor is Catholic, both are committed to science, but they conceded that sometimes astonishing things happen.

We Catholics call them miracles and Shawn Gerleman is certain that Avery was the recipient of one. He recognizes God's hand at work in the little coincidences along the way. Him discovering a biography of Father Kapaun at his grandmother's home. How years after Avery walked out the door of Wesley, he was rummaging through some boxes and found his notes on intercessory prayer scribbled on a church bulletin that he had found in a pew of his chapel. Shawn flipped it over and saw that it had been printed by the Father Kapaun Guild.

"I absolutely think that it's a miracle," he said. "I shake my head recalling the whole experience. The *thump, thump, thump* of the ventilators. The crushing bad news."

Especially now. Shawn Gerleman has returned to Wesley Medical Center, where he is a chaplain resident at a place he knows so well. For the past thirteen months, Shawn has made the ninety-minute commute five days a week from his home in Emporia to Wichita. Like Avery, he was pulled there by his faith and the spirit of Father Kapaun to minister to people who are suffering no matter what their religion.

"We experienced those struggles and that suffering," said Shawn. "I hear that *thump, thump, thump* of the ventilator and sit with family members whose loved ones are in terrible pain or told they are dying. I know what that's like. We know what that's like."

Talitha koum. Little girl, arise. The Gerlemans got a miracle.

Shawn absolutely believes Father Kapaun is a saint. He hopes and prays the Vatican eventually recognizes him as one. And if they do not? Shawn offers a more practical than philosophical opinion. One that is a bedrock belief of his embrace of intercessory prayer.

"Father Kapaun is in heaven along with a whole lot of other people that will never be recognized as a saint, from my grandfather to your mom and dad and all the other good people we know who are in heaven. I thank Father Kapaun every day and I pray to other people who are not going to become saints. It doesn't mean that they are not close to God. And I know that I can use all the help I can get."

17

In December of 2019, Dr. Ambrosi called Father Hotze and told him that the Congregation for the Causes of Saints was going to meet on March 10, 2020, in Rome to decide if the documents that he had compiled, and that Ambrosi had sculpted, sufficiently proved that Father Kapaun had lived a life of heroic virtue and sanctity. If the cardinals and bishops deemed so, his case would be presented to Pope Francis, who would decide whether Kapaun should be bestowed with the title of Venerable, thus climbing to the second step on the four-step ladder to becoming a Saint.

Both agreed this was terrific news. They were heartened that the cause of Father Kapaun was gaining momentum. After all, it was just four years prior—on November 9, 2015—that Bishop Carl A. Kemme of Wichita traveled to the Vatican with a delegation to officially present the documents to the then prefect of the Congregation for the Causes of Saints, Cardinal Angelo Amato. In the deliberate calculus of Saint-making, Ambrosi assured Father Hotze the process was progressing at warp speed. Both Ambrosi and Father Hotze anticipated that the congregation would accept their work positively and Pope Francis would proclaim Father Kapaun Venerable. With good reason—not only were they confident that Father Kapaun was saint material and they had made their case, but they also were aware that causes rarely got stopped at this level. In fact, neither of them nor the Jesuit postulator, Father Pascual Cebollada Silvestre, could recall a cause being rejected at this stage. It was always a lack of miracles that stalled or snuffed out the candidacies of would-be saints.

Ambrosi, the miracle hunter, believed that was not going to be a problem. He had the two miracles in his pocket and was eager to get the first one, Chase Kear, before the congregation's medical panel. It was written up and ready to go and, he believed, it was as strong as any of the others that he had successfully presented. Chase would lead to the beatification of Father Kapaun. If not, the remarkable recovery of Avery Gerleman would lead him through the door to beatification. In Ambrosi's opinion, Avery's case was the equivalent of a slam dunk. It was meticulously documented and enhanced by the testimony of two non-Catholic doctors who say unequivocally that they witnessed a miracle.

The day before the meeting—on March 9, 2020—the

Italian government locked down the country, telling its residents to stay inside. The world was under siege by a mysterious and deadly virus called the coronavirus. It first appeared in January, starting in Wuhan, China, and now was ripping through Europe, Iran, and the United States. The discussion of Father Kapaun in the Congregation for the Causes of Saints was canceled as the Vatican, and the world, immediately turned its attention to what was a growing pandemic. There is no need to tell you about the countless (and still counting) lives lost—parents, spouses, relatives, and friends. We are all living through it. Many have lost jobs. Our economies have been wrecked and, in the United States, the enmity, distrust, suspicion, and rage dividing us from one another spilled out into the streets in the form of protests after a white police officer in Minneapolis put a knee on the neck of an African American man in his custody by the name of George Floyd. He held it there for nearly nine minutes, killing Floyd. For weeks afterward, protest marches and rallies took place in big cities and small towns across the country. Black Lives Matter became a rallying cry for a diverse crowd of all ages, and meaningful conversations about social justice were taking place for the first time in decades if not centuries.

On the evening of March 27, 2020, Pope Francis acknowledged that our faith was being tested as the world was seemingly coming apart. He appeared in St. Peter's Square to deliver an Urbi et Orbi address on the coronavirus and Jesus calming the storm. It happened to be the deadliest day of the coronavirus in Italy, with 919 new deaths reported in the previous twenty-four hours to push the country's death toll past 9,100. The previous day, the United States became the home to the most confirmed cases in the world and counted more than 1,500 deaths. The number of deaths in the United States subsequently would grow exponentially to more than 160,000 by mid-August 2020.

The pope was alone, beneath a canopy to shield him from the rain that was coming down and bouncing off the ancient cobblestones of the square. He was bathed in the blue lights of police cruisers as the police enforced the lockdown across Rome. Pope Francis knew Italy, the world, was anxious and terrified. The Gospel of St. Mark, verses 4:35–41, about the miracle at sea, had just been read. They tell the story about how Jesus and his disciples were in a boat that got caught in a squall. Jesus was sleeping soundly in the stern, but his disciples panicked and were afraid the boat would be overturned and that they would drown. They woke Jesus from his sleep. He rose and calmed the winds. Then he stilled the waves. But Jesus was unsettled: "Why are you so afraid? Do you still have no faith?"

In his homily, Pope Francis wanted us to recognize ourselves in this story.

"Thick darkness has gathered over our squares, our streets, and our cities; it has taken over our lives, filling everything with a deafening silence and a distressing void, that stops everything as it passes by; we feel it in the air, we notice in people's gestures, their glances give them away," the pope began. "We find ourselves afraid and lost. Like the disciples in the Gospel we were caught off guard by an unexpected, turbulent storm. We have realized that we are on the same boat, all of us fragile and disoriented, but at the same time important and needed, all of us called to row together, each of us in need of comforting the other."

In seventeen hundred words or so, Pope Francis asked us to look inside ourselves and identify what we believe. He tried to reassure us that we would be safe.

"Like the disciples, we will experience that, with him on board, there will be no shipwreck. Because this is God's strength: turning to the good everything that happens to us, even the bad things. He brings serenity into our storms, because with God life never dies."

He admonished us—for our greed, our vanity, and our selfishness.

"We did not stop at your reproach to us, we were not shaken awake by wars or injustice across the world, nor did we listen to the cry of the poor or of our ailing planet. We carried on regardless, thinking we would stay healthy in a world that was sick."

But finally, Pope Francis reminded us not to be afraid.

"By his cross we have been saved in order to embrace hope and let it strengthen and sustain all measures and all possible avenues for helping us protect ourselves and others. Embracing the Lord in order to embrace hope: that is the strength of faith, which frees us from fear and gives us hope."

Watching at home in New York City, my son remote-learning, my wife making Zoom calls, and all of us, frankly, knowing that more terrible and trying times were ahead, I was grateful that I had spent this time with Father Emil Kapaun, examining his life and, yes, praying to him.

What Pope Francis was telling us to do—to turn away from panic and terror and toward God—is what Father Kapaun had done on the battlefields and in the prison camps of Korea. He saw the lost looks and terrible darkness in the faces of his fellow GI's and reassured them that together they were going to make their way through their tribulation. When they were hungry, weak, and ill, he came up with imaginary coffee to drink and rib-eye steaks to taste, turning the bad into good. He scavenged food for them, engineered tools out of scrap to give them the tiniest bit of comfort, and shook them awake from their selfish ways when they wanted to hoard food or be cruel to one another. Camp No. 5 was a sick and twisted prison, but with prayer and defiance, kindness and love, Father Kapaun made it survivable for many of his men. He demonstrated God's strength at every turn. His example showed them the strength that they could receive by turning to God. He did not care what faith his men were—Jewish, Muslim, or Baptist—but he did want them to embrace it, to free themselves from fear. To find hope.

Did Father Kapaun imitate the life of Christ? Absolutely, right down to forgiving his Chinese captors and then asking them for forgiveness even though they had made his and his men's daily existence a living hell. His final words were a request: "Forgive me?" They were uttered to the officer in charge at the Death House door, Father Kapaun knowing full well that he would never walk out of there.

Is Father Kapaun a saint? To the GI's he served with, he sure the hell is. He is a saint to the Kears and the Gerlemans, who still have their son and daughter after they prayed to him. There are tens of thousands—perhaps even hundreds of thousands—of people from Kansas and beyond who pray, "Father Kapaun, help me," and ask him to intercede in their troubles. Before 1588, when the Congregation of Rites and Ceremonies was created, that alone would have made him a Saint. He would have been just as qualified as the giant ferryman of legend, Saint Christopher, or Saint Jude, the patron saint of lost causes, whom no one is sure ever really existed.

For now, Father Kapaun remains a Servant of God and stuck on the runway to sainthood. It is a title doled out by an imperfect Church that is run by imperfect men who many centuries ago wanted to have more control over who was named a Saint. They wanted to choose what men and women would represent their brand. The road to sainthood is expensive and its steep entry fee only buys would-be Saints a ping-pong ball in the lottery of divinity. The historians, theologians, cardinals, bishops, and doctors are rightly rigorous, and they perform their duties in good faith.

But as the fast-tracked canonizations of Pope John Paul II and Mother Teresa and the induction of the one-miracle-shy Pope John XXIII show, public relations and good politics play important roles in the decision-making process. So do geopolitics and good business. More Latin American Saints are made so as to hold the line until more priests can be deployed to the once-Catholic stronghold that is now losing ground to the evangelicals. Africa and Asia have been identified as targets for the naming of new Saints to gain converts.

Even Pope Francis has bent the rules of canonization. He has added six new Saints, including a cofounder of the Jesuit order, Father Peter Faber, by invoking "equivalent canonization." It's a concept that allows a pope to waive the normal rules in cases where the person has been a Venerable for a long time and has a reputation for miraculous intercession. In other words, no documented miracles are needed.

Monsignor Sarno, America's man in the congregation, has explained that the requirement to have miracles for sainthood is an ecclesiastical law—not a divine one.

"It's not that a miracle is divinely required," he said.

"What is divinely required is holiness of life. By martyrdom or holiness of life, these Saints have attained the goal of heaven, by following Christ more closely. The key thing about sainthood is imitating their lives, not looking for a miracle."

By the standard offered by Monsignor Sarno, then, Father Kapaun is already a Saint.

Perhaps it's true that an American priest, and a military man to boot, is not exactly a fashionable choice for sainthood these days. But that choice would actually be a healing and thoroughly modern one. There are wars and acts of terrorism going on in all corners of the world. Crippling poverty and hunger have taken the lives of children around the globe. Sickness and suffering have spread their wings through viruses we've never seen and familiar diseases that we cannot defeat.

Service, courage, and forgiveness—for all—were the hallmarks of Father Kapaun's life, three attributes that are in short supply these days. The Catholic Church needs to serve all its people regardless of their sexual preference or politics. It could use some courage to meaningfully address its sexual abuse problem and turn over offenders to law enforcement authorities. There are different levels of forgiveness that we all need to navigate. Can abuse victims forgive their abusers? Can African Americans forgive the white police officers who violate their rights? It is hard enough for us to forgive friends or spouses, family members and coworkers for everyday transgressions. Forgiveness is a virtue in short supply. If we are to live a Christlike life, we need to employ it more often in matters big and small.

Yes, Father Kapaun lived a life worth imitating.

Father Hotze understood the impatience of Father Kapaun's fellow prisoners of war. He shows patience to Kansans and devotees to the chaplain who cannot understand the slow-grinding gears of the Vatican's Saint-making machinery. Father Hotze is in it for the long haul. Even if he is not alive to see the canonization of Father Kapaun, he believes the reward will be worth the wait.

"He was just an average guy. He was just a poor Kansas farm boy. He had nothing, and he was able to use what little he had in service to others," he said. "If he becomes a Saint, then there's hope for each and every one of us to be a saint."

I will wait, too, and hope against hope that I am still around when Father Kapaun is finally made a Saint.

Until then, he will remain in my prayers.

I pray that I remain in his.

ACKNOWLEDGMENTS

Writing a book is a process of discovery and when it is all said and done, I am better off for learning about other worlds and, in the case of *The Saint Makers*, ultimately about myself. I'm better off for this book and need to thank those who made me so.

I appreciate the time and care Father John Hotze and Dr. Andrea Ambrosi put into sharing their histories and insights on Father Kapaun and the Saint-making process with me. Chase Kear was candid about his injury and recovery and his continuing struggles with being a Miracle Man. Avery Gerleman and her father, Shawn, are convincing advocates for the power of prayer. In Rome, Monsignor Robert Sarno and Father Pascual Cebollada Silvestre were generous in helping me understand a centuries-old system of deciding who is truly a saint. This book would not have come together without all of these folks' patience, honesty, and good humor. Thank you, one and all.

ACKNOWLEDGMENTS

Talk about patience, Brant Rumble, my editor at Hachette Books, showed infinite reserves with me. His keen and deft insights made this book better. In fact, I am grateful for the effort of the whole Hachette team— Michael Clark, Mike van Mantgem, Mollie Weisenfeld, Michael Barrs, and Sarah Falter—for sending *The Saint Makers* into the world. I also need to thank Mauro DiPreta for encouraging me to leave the fields of play and racetrack for a spell to explore my other interests. Bob Curran has newspapers in his pedigree. He kindly and bravely read the initial drafts of the book to make sure I was factually correct and stylistically defensible.

These folks shared their thoughts about faith and the Catholic Church and were key to the reporting and writing of this book—Bob Berner, Naka Nathaniel, Drew Jubera, and Craig Malloy. And many thanks to Father James Martin for helping me rediscover prayer and urging me to wrestle with my faith on the page. I also need to thank all the priests, nuns, Jesuits, and lay teachers at the Catholic schools of my youth as well as the ones now laying the foundation of faith for my son.

I am blessed to have good friends here in New York as well as Kansas City and Texas and other random places. You offer wise and not-so-wise advice, but mostly you make me think, laugh, and feel. Thank you.

I am bountifully blessed by a large, often unruly family of Drapes and Kennedys, which includes in-laws and out-laws, and nieces and nephews. You are not only big fun, but you have shown Jack Drape what the warm embrace of family means.

I love you all.

Mary Kennedy, I owe you everything. Jack, you got the best Mom ever and, because of you both, I am the luckiest man in the world.

A NOTE ON SOURCES

The Saint Makers was an interesting book to put together because it was a mash-up of a biography, journalism, and memoir. The reporting sent me down a variety of rabbit holes—the Korean War, Vatican policy and politics, and the history of the Catholic Church in America. I leaned on academic papers written by economists and books written by Korean War and Church historians. Two previous biographies written about Father Kapaun and documents amassed by Father Hotze and available at catholicdioceseofwichita.org/father-kapaun ensured that I was not putting words in the chaplain's or anybody else's mouth.

A NOTE ON SOURCES

SELECTED BIBLIOGRAPHY

Associated Press. "New Abuse Suits Could Cost Church Over $4B." December 2, 2019.

Barro, Robert J., and Rachel M. McCleary and Alexander McQuoid. "Economics of Sainthood (A Preliminary Investigation)." Research paper, February 2010.

Bonnefoy, Pascale, and Austin Ramzy. "Pope's Defense of Chilean Bishop in Sex Abuse Scandal Causes Outrage." *New York Times*, January 19, 2018.

Briggs, Bill. *The Third Miracle: An Ordinary Man, a Medical Mystery, and a Trial of Faith.* New York: Crown, 2010.

Calmes, Jackie. "Medal of Honor Awarded to Korean War Chaplain." *New York Times*, April 11, 2013.

De Zutter, Albert. "Msgr. Kearney Dies of Injuries from Accident." *Catholic Key*, April 2003.

Dowe, Raymond Michael, Jr. "The Ordeal of Chaplain Kapaun." *Saturday Evening Post*, January 16, 1954.

Garcia, Ahiza. "Vatican Inc.: 5 Facts About the Business of the Catholic Church." CNN.com, September 24, 2015.

Horowitz, Jason, and Elizabeth Dias. "Pope Francis Ends Landmark Sex Abuse Meeting with Strong Words, but Few Actions." *New York Times*, February 24, 2019.

Horowitz, Jason, and Elisabeth Povoledo. "Vatican Hopes Meeting on Child Sex Abuse Will Be a Turning Point." *New York Times*, February 18, 2019.

Kosloski, Philip. "The Saint-Makers: Why Did Popes John Paul II, Benedict and Francis Canonize So Many Saints?" Aleteia.org, November 1, 2016.

Likpka, Michael, and Tim Townsend. "Papal Saints: Once a Given, Now Extremely Rare." Pew Research Center, April 24, 2014.

Lockwood, Patricia. *Priestdaddy: A Memoir.* New York: Riverhead Books, 2017.

Maher, William L. *A Shepherd in Combat Boots: Chaplain Emil Kapaun of the 1st Cavalry Division.* Shippensburg, PA: White Mane, 1997.

Manning, Kathleen. "How Many Saints Are There?" *U.S. Catholic*, November 2013.

McElwee, Joshua. "Francis Accepts Two More Chilean Bishops' Resignations in Continuing Abuse Fallout." *National Catholic Reporter*, June 28, 2018.

Morrison, Kristopher. "Wealth of Roman Catholic Church Impossible to Calculate." *National Post*, March 9, 2013.

A NOTE ON SOURCES

Nathaniel, Naka. "I Stood Up in Mass and Confronted My Priest. You Should, Too." *New York Times*, August 23, 2018,

Nuzzi, Gianluigi. *Merchants in the Temple: Inside Pope Francis's Secret Battle Against Corruption in the Vatican.* New York: Henry Holt, 2015.

O'Connell, Gerard. "Pope Francis Marks Jesuit Social Justice Initiative Anniversary." *America*, November 7, 2019.

Sprows Cummings, Kathleen. *A Saint of Our Own: How the Quest for a Holy Hero Helped Catholics Become American.* Chapel Hill: University of North Carolina Press, 2019.

Thavis, John. "John XXIII & the Missing Miracle." *Legatus*, June 2, 2014.

Thavis, John. *The Vatican Prophecies: Investigating Supernatural Signs, Apparitions, and Miracles in the Modern Age.* New York: Viking, 2015.

Vargas, Elizabeth, and Donna Hunter. "Miracle of Faith: The Work of a Saint?" ABC News, April 2, 2010.

Wenzl, Roy. "Diocese Passes Kapaun Case for Sainthood to Vatican Investigator." *Wichita Eagle*, July 2, 2011.

Wenzl, Roy, and Travis Heying. *The Miracle of Father Kapaun: Priest, Soldier and Korean War Hero.* San Francisco: Ignatius Press, 2015.

INDEX

INDEX

INDEX

INDEX

INDEX

liberation theology, 158, 164
lice infestation, 107–108
The Lives of the Fathers, Martyrs, and Other Principal Saints (Butler), 22–23
Lives of the Saints (Butler), 22–23
Lockwood, Patricia, 136–137

Maciel (priest), 26
MacKillop, Mary (nun), 143–144
Martin, James J. (priest), 63–65, 135
martyrs, 24, 28–29, 155–156, 165–166
Martyrs of Otranto, 28–29
Mayo, Walt, 83, 92, 95–97, 116–117, 119, 123
McCarrick, Theodore (priest), 194
McClain, William "Moose," 124
McCool, Felix, 116
McGreevy, Robert, 120, 128, 185–187, 190, 197
Medal of Honor, 128–130, 180, 210
military service, Father Kapaun's
  broadening his constituency, 66–68
  as a calling, 68–69
  Chinese attack at Unsan, 80–92
  conducting Mass in Korea, 76–79
  Father Hotze's fact-finding mission, 47–48
  Father Kapaun's calling, 42–43
  as obstacle to Father Kapaun's canonization, 34
  valor and heroism, 2–3, 44–45, 78, 121–122, 130–132, 182–183
Miller, Herb, 84–85, 128–130, 132, 210
Mills, Arthur, 72
Mindszenty, József (cardinal), 168, 170
miracles
  Avery Gerleman, 211–223, 225
  belief in, 198–199
  canonization requirements, 19, 24–26, 173
  Chase Kear, 199–210, 225
  equivalent canonization, 231–232
  essence of sainthood, 18

evolution of the canonization process, 23
Father Kapaun's, 182–183
of John Henry Newman, 168–169
people wanting to connect to, 208–210
reduction of the requirement, 173
requirements for Father Kapaun's cause, 12–13
Saint Theodora, 175
waiving the requirement for, 26
Monegundis (saint), 20
Moscoso, Emilia (priest), 155–156, 159–160
Mother Teresa, 164, 231
Mount Saint Mary's Seminary, Emmitsburg, Maryland, 5, 10
Mug, Mary Theodosia (nun), 175
Mundelein, George (cardinal), 30
Murphy, Joseph, 61

Nardella, Ralph, 101, 108, 111–112, 116–118, 120, 126
Nathaniel, Naka, 188–190, 197
Neumann, John (bishop), 31
Newman, John Henry (saint), 168–169, 175
Nieto, Manuel García (priest), 155, 161–162
Norris, Kathleen, 146–147
Nuzzi, Gianluigi, 177, 179

Obama, Barack, 128–130, 180
O'Brien, Phil, 130–133
O'Connell, William Henry (cardinal), 30
O'Connor, Joseph, 74, 79
Olmsted, Thomas (bishop), 8–10
Openibo, Veronica (nun), 195–196
Orwell, George, 49

pandemic, 226
Pardon My Take (podcast), 137
patriarchy, challenging, 52
Paul III (pope), 152

INDEX

INDEX